PORTRAIT OF
WINDERMERE

Portrait of
WINDERMERE

by

Christopher D. Taylor

ROBERT HALE · LONDON

ISBN 0 7090 0924 0

Robert Hale Limited
Clerkenwell House
Clerkenwell Green
London EC1R 0 HT

For Paul and Ruth
and all other mountain goats

Photoset in North Wales by
Derek Doyle & Associates, Mold, Clwyd
Printed in Great Britain by
St Edmundsbury Press, Bury St Edmunds, Suffolk
Bound by Woolnough Bookbinding Ltd

Contents

Illustrations

Remains of the ironworks at Backbarrow
The blast furnace, Backbarrow
Stott Park bobbin mill, Finsthwaite
High Dam, Finsthwaite Heights
The Round House on Belle Isle

Between pages 144 and 145

Storrs Temple
Wray Castle
A corner of old Hawkshead
Wordsworth Street, Hawkshead
The Old Grammar School, Hawkshead
The Windermere Ferry and Claife Heights
The Windermere Hotel
Belsfield
Moss Eccles Tarn, Claife Heights
St Martin's, Bowness
Boats moored at Bowness Bay
Sailing-boats moored near Ferry Nab
The *Swan* off Belle Isle
Old fishermen's huts and Sepulchre Hill, Bowness

MAPS AND DIAGRAMS

AUTHOR'S ACKNOWLEDGEMENTS

Like the landscape it describes, this book has been in the making for many years, and I am grateful to all those who have assisted me during that time.

In many ways the research has been a family effort, and above all, thanks are due to my wife, Jenifer, who has encouraged me throughout, and to my children who have walked many miles exploring the area with me on foot. To them this book is dedicated.

Christopher D. Taylor

Bowness-on-Windermere

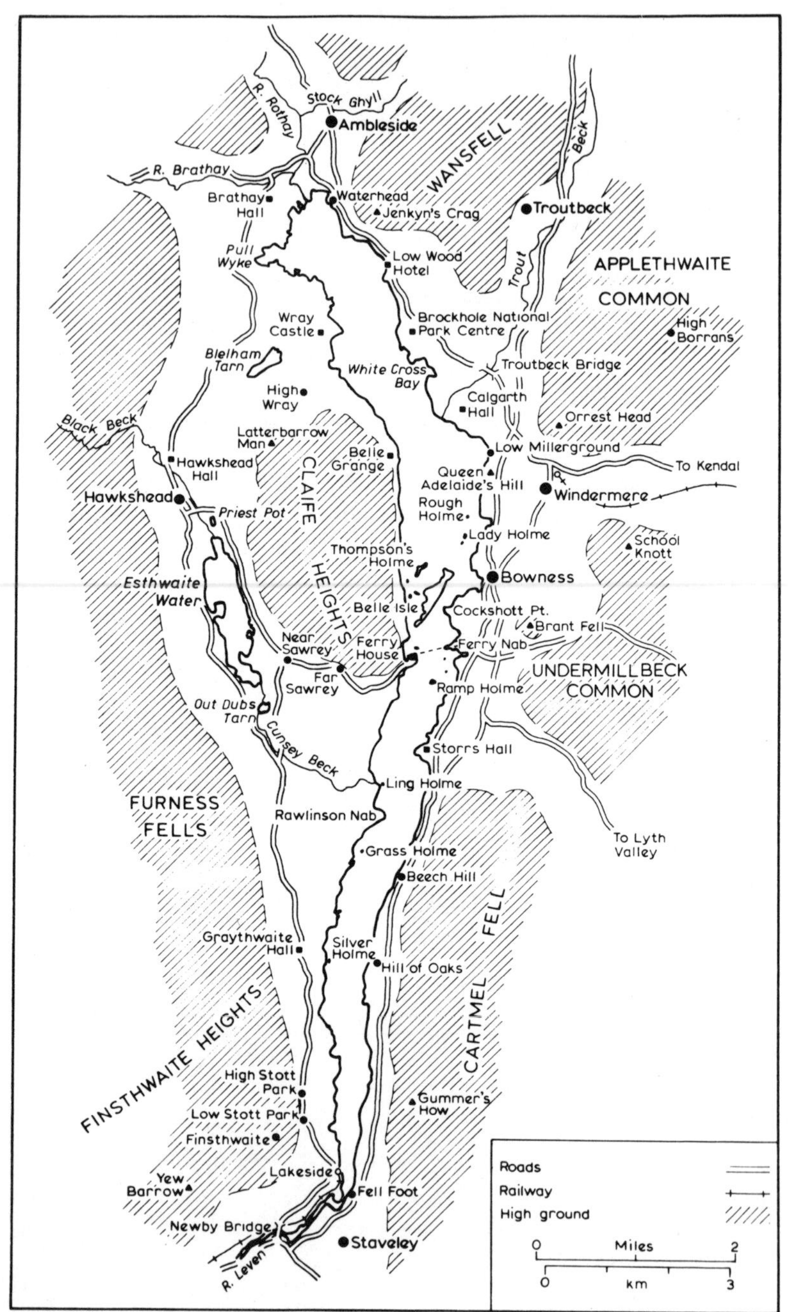

Windermere and the surrounding fells

Introduction

Many excellent volumes have been written about the Lake District, but surprisingly little has been written about the lakes themselves.

Portrait of Windermere sets out to explore just *one* of them: a lake which is undoubtedly the most well-known and probably the most well-loved in England; a lake about which much has been recorded but whose complete story has never been told.

But this is not just the story of Windermere itself, for just as it is impossible to view the lake without looking beyond to the surrounding fells, so it would be very difficult to write about the lake without constantly referring to the ways in which the surrounding landscape has shaped, moulded and shared in its evolution. Windermere cannot be separated from its landscape, and we should make no attempt to do so.

The result is a portrait of a Lakeland landscape, the story of the formation of the longest lake in England, together with the woods and fellsides, the roads and communities which together make up the unique landscape of Southern Lakeland. It is an exciting story, ranging over thousands – even millions – of years, with volcanoes and glaciers, Romans and Vikings, stage-coaches and flying boats each making their contribution to the development of the scenery in the Windermere area.

For the visitor who has only glimpsed Windermere from the shores of Bowness Bay, or from the main road near the Low Wood Hotel, it is hoped that this introduction will stimulate an appetite to explore the area more closely. For the student who is seeking to understand the Lakeland landscape in greater depth, the book describes an area which contains a wealth of fascinating geomorphological and historical detail. For those whose love of

Windermere has already prompted them to explore the area more carefully on foot – or by boat – it is hoped that this account may further add to their understanding of the beauty which is evident all around them in the Windermere landscape.

1

The Windermere Landscape

Perhaps it should not come as too much of a surprise to discover that the mountains of the Lake District invariably overshadow the lakes themselves. After all, climbers and fell-walkers have for many years adopted the Lake District as their second home. Even for the vast majority of casual visitors, approaching the area by road from the south, their first impression of the region is dominated by the sheer grandeur of the fells. As the motorist reaches the summit of the deep limestone cutting at the northern end of the Kendal bypass, the panorama opening before his eyes is framed by the distant hills of the Kentmere range, laid out before him like a giant caterpillar. Each one of these seeming giants – Potter Fell, Green Quarter Fell, Shipman Knotts and Kentmere Pike – rises up steeply from the floor of the Kentmere valley, each summit higher than the previous one as they reach out towards the far horizon. These impressive fells provide the scenic backcloth as, beyond the roundabout, the main road gently winds up and down over the rocky low ground which is characteristic of this part of the Lake District.

Beyond the village of Staveley the road keeps to the valley floor, passing close beneath the seemingly impregnable face of Reston Scar before it recommences its switchback ride over the low, hummocky mounds of glacial moraine. Each new summit provides a fresh vista of small, walled pastures and distant peaks as the road gradually gains height beyond the tiny settlement of Ings and climbs over the southern flank of Banner Rigg, a blunt mass of rock bordering the road to the north. Beyond the crest of the ridge the highway drops down once again before climbing steeply up the western flank of Orrest Head, close by Alice Howe. And then – suddenly – taking us quite by surprise as we reach the brow of the hill, there she is – stretched out before us, to left and to right, like a jewel shining in the sunlight. *This* is Windermere – the longest lake in England and, to many, the most beautiful. Like a long silver ribbon she winds gently beneath us, the wooded slopes of Claife Heights rising steeply from her far bank, while beyond, the summits of Coniston Old Man, Wetherlam and the Langdale Pikes provide a fitting backcloth to the scene.

However many times I pass this spot, the startling view always takes me by surprise. It provides a fleeting glimpse – and then is gone; a breath-taking introduction to a magnificent landscape; a view just sufficient to whet the appetite to explore more closely the lake which is now fast disappearing into its deep, wooded trough as the road tumbles round the sharp bend into Windermere village.

Professor Wilson, one-time local author and academic, said of the view from nearby Orrest Head, 'There is not such another prospect in all England.' Many would agree with him, despite the changes which have occurred since he surveyed the scene from his home, early in the nineteenth century. William Wordsworth, having travelled along the same road from Kendal, described this view in his poem 'The Prelude':

> Standing alone, as from a rampart's edge,
> I overlooked the bed of Windermere,
> Like a vast river, stretching in the sun.
> With exultation, at my feet I saw
> Lake, islands, promontories, gleaming bays,
> A universe of Nature's fairest forms
> Proudly revealed with instantaneous burst,
> Magnificent, and beautiful, and gay.

What is it that has caused countless others to echo Wilson's praise and has stirred the emotions of generations of travellers following in Wordsworth's footsteps? Why, when viewed not only from Orrest Head but also from Gummer's How or Brant Fell, from Claife Heights or Wansfell Pike, is the landscape of Windermere so magnificently appealing?

The answer lies partly in the *scale* of the scenery. Windermere, although the longest lake in England, is relatively narrow and compact. From the iron age hill fort on the summit of

Allen Knott, the whole 10½-mile-long sheet of water can be seen in a single glance. A comparable view elsewhere across an endless expanse of lake or ocean may have a certain awe-inspiring majesty of its own, but water alone rarely provides a really pleasing and balanced picture. Only when the water forms part of a more varied landscape, its calm, flat sheet complementing the rugged and irregular valley sides, does water become irresistibly attractive. On a still, clear day, the surface of the lake becomes a mirror, reflecting the summits of the Cumbrian mountains between its rocky islands. Looking north across Bowness Bay, the sparkling water reflects the giant peaks of Fairfield and Dollywaggon Pike, each not only rising three thousand feet above the water but also, apparently, plunging three thousand feet down into its cavernous depths. Undoubtedly, without the neighbouring fells, Windermere itself would be dull. As it is, the steep wooded slopes which tower above the water, and often reach down to the lake's edge, add a dimension to the landscape which sets it in a class apart from much more extensive tracts of water.

Then there is the lake itself. Windermere has what may be described as an extremely attractive 'waterscape'. Unlike the artificial and regular shore-lines of many man-made lakes and reservoirs, Windermere has a wonderful natural variety along its shores. The lakeside is enhanced by innumerable small bays and inlets, some secluded by wooded banks, others opening out onto gently sloping pastures. The view from each of these nooks and crannies has its own individual charm. Sometimes the panorama opens up down a long reach of the lake; at other times the trees, hanging down towards the water, provide a tight picture-frame, directing the gaze to a closer view of a neighbouring wooded shore. Or perhaps the vista is interrupted by one of the many small islands, dotted about almost at random, which peep out from beneath the mirror and break the visual calm of the water's flat surface. Some of these islands are hardly large enough for a single tree to gain a footing, whilst others attain several acres and rise steeply from the water's edge. The largest, Belle Isle, is the only inhabited island, its attractive round house having been the home of the Curwen family since the eighteenth century. Undoubtedly it is this tremendous variety of scenery within such a small area that makes Windermere one of the most attractive landscapes in the whole of the Lake District.

And yet, while it is often regarded as the most popular of the Lakeland landscapes, the Windermere area is far from being a typical Lake District landscape. Southern Lakeland, in which Windermere lies, has a charm of its own which is far removed from the appeal of the more barren northerly districts. Even to the casual visitor, the scenery surrounding Windermere appears much smoother and gentler than the harsh, rugged landscape of the Central Fells. Largely because of geological differences, the Windermere area has lower relief, and its summits are less angular than those of the Central Lake District. This fact is most easily perceived if one approaches Windermere from the south, travelling along the whole length of the lake from Newby Bridge to Ambleside.

In its most southerly reach near Lakeside, Windermere is flanked by low fells whose gentle lower slopes spread out across the valley floor before descending meekly to the water's edge. Most of these fells are below eight hundred feet, and only Gummer's How – a seeming giant in this context – overtops the thousand-foot contour. As far north as Bowness Bay the lake shore is overlooked by these low fells, forming the gently rolling Silurian country of Southern Lakeland. Only beyond Rayrigg Woods and Queen Adelaide's Hill does the landscape begin to alter. A variation in rock type heralds the change to a steeper, more rugged and higher landscape typical of the Central Mountainous District, and the gentler slopes of Southern Lakeland are soon left behind. To the north-east, the view along the Troutbeck valley is dominated by the angular peaks of Yoke, Froswick and Ill Bell, each well above two thousand feet, while in the west, beyond Belle Grange, the pointed summits of the Langdale Pikes become clearly visible behind Wray Castle. Directly to the north, Ambleside is overshadowed by the razor-sharp ridges of the Fairfield Horseshoe, leading ultimately to the summit of Helvellyn at 3,118 feet.

In a very short distance as we have travelled north, the scenery has changed from the gentle, wooded slopes of the Windermere area to the bleak, rocky crags of the Central Lake District. Without question, most of the other lakes – Thirlmere,

Buttermere and Derwent Water, for example – belong wholeheartedly to this Central Region, but, while having a foothold in the mountainous core, Windermere undoubtedly belongs to the lower country of the Silurian foothills.

In many other ways Windermere's landscape differs from the scenery which is typical of the central part of the Lake District. Unlike the wilder areas of the Cumbrian Mountains, most of the scenery surrounding Windermere clearly bears the stamp of man. Indeed, the landscape of the Windermere area is almost totally a man-made landscape, a landscape which has been moulded and fashioned over the centuries by countless generations of peasants and landowners and which is still being actively changed today by the impact of man on the local environment.

Perhaps the most obvious manifestations of the hand of man on the Windermere landscape are the numerous plantations of larch and spruce, planted since the seventeenth century, which sweep down the valley sides often to the water's edge. These trees were often planted as much for their aesthetic contribution to the landscape as for their commercial value, and the extent of planting has caused many to regard Windermere as the most artificially landscaped of all the lakes. On the west bank these plantations almost completely blanket the steep slopes of Claife Heights opposite Bowness Bay, whilst on the east shore, the lower slopes to the north of Gummer's How are dominated by the mixed woodlands of Great Tower Plantation and Haws Wood. Further west, even larger stands of spruce and larch have been planted in recent years by the Forestry Commission based at Grizedale.

It is not only the coniferous plantations, however, which have contributed to the individuality of the Windermere landscape. Towards the southern end of the lake, the slopes of Cartmel Fell and High Furness have, for centuries, been covered predominantly by deciduous trees. This coppiced woodland, comprising oak, hazel, birch and alder – among other species – was for many hundreds of years the primary source of charcoal for the local iron-smelters of the Backbarrow Gorge. The trees were felled every fifteen to twenty years and then allowed to re-generate, resulting in numerous trunks springing up from the one root – the typical feature of coppiced woodland. A careful search among the tangled undergrowth near Windermere's shores will sometimes reveal the crumbling remains of an ancient charcoal pitstead, long overgrown but still easily recognized by its characteristic flat floor. This timber was also grown for use by the local woodland industries – basket making and bobbin mills being just two examples of the local trades which relied on the woodlands bordering Windermere for their basic raw materials.

Outside these man-made woodlands, the slopes are often covered with bracken, the bright green fronds which burst forth in the spring, choking the slope with a dense matting of leaves until the bracken fades in the autumn and falls away to leave a ragged carpet of crisp brown stems. Yet even the extensive growth of bracken on the valley sides is not entirely natural, as in past centuries this growth was actively encouraged by the local manufacturers of potash soap – an essential product in the fulling of local hand-made woollen cloth. Today the renewed growth of bracken on the hillside pastures is often one of the first indications that a fellside has been over-grazed.

Where the bracken has not been allowed to take over, the grassy slopes are often covered by springy turf, mosses and lichens. Here again, the vegetation has been extensively modified by the influence of man ever since the Norse settlers of the tenth century began to feed their flocks of sheep on the gently sloping hillsides. Constant grazing by centuries of sheep has maintained a close cover of short-cropped turf, while artificial drainage and manure have steadily improved the quality of the pasture. Where larger hummocks provide shelter, bilberries promise a succulent feast in the summer, while heather gains a footing on the drier areas such as the cracks amongst the rocky outcrops.

Not all the vegetation, however, has been introduced or modified by man. Where the ground is well drained on the steeper slopes, numerous species of wild flowers have grown up among the grasses. Here, charlock, coltsfoot and tiny tormentil bend their golden heads, together with heath bedstraw and sheep sorrel, while in the poorly drained hollows, white, feathery bog cotton grass and springy green sphagnum take over. Even the carefully maintained valley pastures of Troutbeck are covered in the spring by a carpet of wild buttercups. By the lake shore, the small drooping heads of wild blue violets, yellow primroses and purple foxgloves often provide a touch of colour in a sheltered nook, while in the spring, the lakeside woods at Millerground are covered by a dense, gilded carpet of dancing wild daffodils. Even within a few feet of the roadside, ox-eye daisies and clumps of white clover, hawkweed and purple loosestrife can be found flowering on the rocky outcrops of Ferry Nab during August. Many of the islands have a hazy carpet of bluebells during the spring, while lilies of the valley grow in profusion on the two islands to the west of Belle Isle which bear that name. Another island – Rampholme – is also named after a wild flower, the sharp-smelling ramp, or wild garlic, which grows there. On the damper patches of the lake shore, sedges and rushes grow in the shallows between moss-covered boulders. Indeed, from the very water's edge to the rocky summits of the fellsides, the visitor who has time to pause and look is entertained by a magnificent variety show of nature's wild beauties.

The Windermere area is not only blessed with a great abundance of flora; it also possesses a wide variety of fauna. Numerous frogs and toads croak in the shallows beside the lake itself, whilst fieldmice, voles and shrews inhabit the hedgerows, and rabbits scamper across the lakeside pastures. In addition to the more common mammals, one or two rarer species are found in the district. Southern Lakeland is one of the few areas in England where the native red squirrel has not yet been replaced by the ubiquitous grey squirrel, brought over from North America as a pet in the nineteenth century. The squirrels perform fantastic feats of acrobatics as they run along the narrow branches and spring from one tall tree to the next. On the ground, a scattered pile of extensively gnawed fir cones is a sure sign that squirrels have recently been enjoying a feast in the vicinity.

Windermere is also one of the few places in Britain where native red deer can be found roaming wild. The woodlands on the western shore provide the best habitat for these animals, and a herd of red deer inhabit the Forestry Commission's plantations at Grizedale. The numbers are strictly controlled by culling, the poorer specimens being picked out to maintain a strong breeding strain. Occasionally the visitor may be fortunate enough to catch a glimpse of a red stag, with its huge antlers – especially if he has waited patiently in the specially constructed and well-camouflaged hides at Grizedale.

Much more common, however, are the smaller roe deer which move gracefully and swiftly through the woods on both sides of the lake. The native roe deer are nocturnal animals and are therefore most likely to be spotted during the evening or early in the morning – especially, perhaps, as they cross the roads on their journey down to the lakeside from the higher slopes. Although free to roam widely, deer will invariably follow the same track down to the water's edge. Where the deer tracks cross the main road from Newby Bridge to Bowness, the motorist is warned of their presence by the characteristic road signs, though it is at night, when the motorist is least expecting it, that the deer are most likely to dart across at these points. Although very attractive to look at, deer can be highly destructive in woodland as the bucks mark out their territory during the mating season by scraping the bark off the trees with their antlers. Hence a number of the commercial woodlands – especially on the western bank – are encircled by tall wire fences to keep out the deer.

The woods are also the home of many birds, bats, butterflies and moths. The jay, with its characteristic clattering call, is one of the most common woodland birds, while the cooing of wood pigeons and the songs of blackbirds can often be heard together with the babbling chatter of robins and tits and the raucous chorus of rooks and crows. By the lake shore and on the lake itself, the black-headed gull is the most common species to be found, while numerous mallard ducks, coots and swans thrive on the abundant titbits offered to them on the popular shores around Waterhead, Bowness Bay and Lakeside.

Windermere, with its reputation as the longest lake in England, is rightly famous because of its sheer size, but it is a less well-known fact that the lake is also extraordinarily deep – being the second deepest of the lakes in the Lake District, after Wastwater. While the middle reach around Bowness Bay and the islands is relatively shallow, the lake has a maximum depth of 209 feet in the northern reaches and a depth of 137 feet in the southern reaches. As the water level is maintained at approximately 129 feet above sea level by the weir at Newby

Bridge, this means that the floor of the lake is some 80 feet *below* sea level at its lowest point – an unusual situation, only adequately explained by the quirks of the Pleistocene glaciation.

Within this huge volume of water there is quite a wide variety of fish. The most common species are the trout – both sea trout and brown trout – and the char, although pike, perch, roach and eels are also frequently caught. The name of the Trout Beck itself suggests that for many centuries the trout have been running up the tributary streams to spawn in September and early October. Indeed, as early as 1615 the King granted fishing rights for 'trowte' and 'salmonds' in the Trout Beck, though no salmon are found in Windermere today.

The char, which in Britain is confined to the cold, deep waters of the Lake District, has been a popular Windermere delicacy for several centuries. Daniel Defoe, writing in the seventeenth century, spoke of 'the fish called charrs [which] come potted to London'. These char pies, made of spiced fish and originally in a pastry case, weighed up to twelve stones when packed in an earthenware pot for transport to the homes of elegant London society.

Trolling for char, by using a line with a large number of hooks on it, was formerly a major occupation on Windermere. Indeed, fishing was the main commercial activity on the lake from at least the thirteenth century down to the middle of the nineteenth century. In 1246 William de Lancaster granted the monks of Furness Abbey the right to use a fishing-boat with twenty nets on Windermere, although twenty-three years earlier the same William had destroyed one of the abbot's boats for fishing illegally!

From the middle of the sixteenth century, the Windermere fisheries were divided into three 'cubbles': the high cubble, stretching from Rothay Bridge to Ecclerigg Crag and including the valuable spawning grounds off Holbeck Ghyll; the middle cubble, stretching south to the ferry and including the spawning grounds north of Rayrigg Hall and Thompson Holme; and the low cubble, covering the southern half of the lake from Ferry Nab to Newby Bridge. The fisheries were owned quite independently of the properties fronting onto the lake shore and were often handed down from one generation to the next. Sometimes the

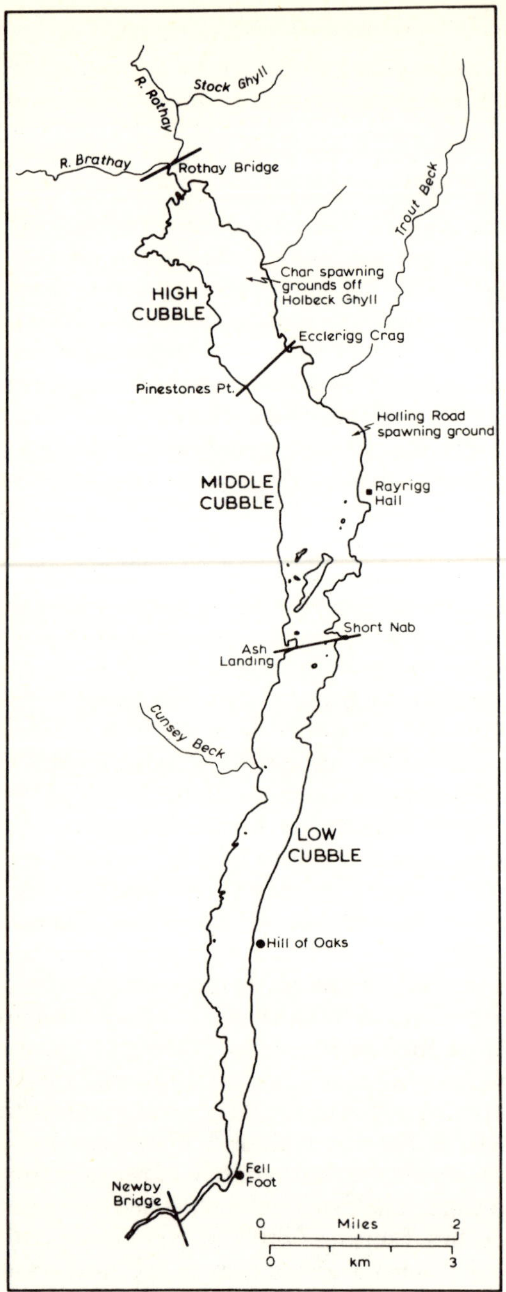

The Windermere Fisheries in the seventeenth century

fishing rights were sold to the highest bidder. In 1693 'Roger Parke younger of Millerground, fisherman' sold 'a moiety or half fishing in the highest and middle cubbles' to John Philipson of Rayrigg. Some of the owners let the fisheries to tenants, who used to catch the trout, pike and perch in long seine nets which were pulled round in a semicircle to trap the shoals and then hauled on board the fishing-boats.

As late as the 1861 Census, eleven men from Bowness and two from Belle Isle were recorded as 'fishermen' or 'boatmen and fishermen'. But by that time overfishing had for many years depleted the stocks, and all netting was stopped for five years by a committee of proprietors in 1863. An Act of Parliament of 1865 established a close season for trout and set up a Board of Conservators who by 1915 had gained control of all the fisheries on Windermere. Netting finally ceased in 1921, bringing to a close seven centuries of commercial fishing.

Long before commercial fishing ceased, however, the proprietors of the Windermere fisheries were already beginning to profit from an alternative source of revenue. In 1793 the proprietors drew up a scale of charges for boats navigating the waters of Windermere. 'A Pleasure Boat, not carrying Goods and Merchandise' was liable to pay, annually, 'the sum of five shillings to the owners of the Fisheries'. Tourism had arrived, and it would not be long before it completely replaced fishing as the main commercial activity on Windermere.

Tourism in the eighteenth century, however, was a very far cry from the commercial tourism we experience today. Up to the middle of the eighteenth century, the Lake District was a little frequented and almost forgotten corner of England, a rough wilderness shunned by the polite, genteel society of the English aristocracy. The Grand Tour of the European continent, with all its cultural delights, was the fashion of the age; a trip to the barren wastes of the barbarous north was definitely *not* 'the done thing'. But the outbreak of the Napoleonic Wars in 1793 on the one hand and the Romanticism of the eighteenth century poets on the other were both to decrease the practicality and the popularity of the Grand Tour and to increase the attraction of the Lake District as a touring centre for the wealthy elite.

In 1748 the first popular account of Windermere appeared in

the *Gentleman's Magazine*. This was followed over the next thirty years by the well-documented journeys of numerous travellers, amongst whose accounts Gray's *Journal*, Gilpin's *Observations*, and Hutchinson's *Excursion* each gained a wide readership. Others of more timid disposition soon followed the pioneers to gaze askance at the awesome precipices of Borrowdale and 'the rugged crags of Biscot-how' (Biskey Howe, above Bowness). Thomas West's *Guide to The Lakes in Cumberland, Westmorland and Lancashire*, published in 1778, was the first in an illustrious line of guidebooks which accompanied the traveller from station to station, ensuring that the newcomer gained the advantage of the best prospects and that the seasoned visitor did not miss the intricate detail encompassed in the extensive panorama.

The popularity of the poetry of William Wordsworth, who himself spent his schooldays at Hawkshead, ensured that the area was no longer a backwater in the eyes of the well-versed. Indeed, Wordsworth's *Guide to the Lakes* is nearly as popular today as when it was first published in 1810 as an Introduction to Wilkinson's *Select Views* of the Lake District. The romantic descriptions of the early Lakeland poets attracted the literary intelligentsia to the Windermere area. Professor Wilson of Elleray and Bishop Watson of Calgarth frequently played host to the Wordsworths, Southey and Hartley Coleridge in the first half of the nineteenth century, while from 1847 to 1876 Harriet Martineau at Ambleside welcomed such literary celebrities as Charlotte Brontë, Charles Dickens and George Eliot, as well as entertaining Gladstone, Disraeli and the Prince of Wales.

Those who settled in the area built themselves large mansions, frequently overlooking the lake and often surrounded by acres of landscaped parkland. Many houses were built along the shores of Windermere at this time. The round house on Belle Isle was built by Thomas English in 1774, while Brathay Hall, built by Mr Law of Old Brathay, was erected in 1788. Dr Watson built Calgarth Park in 1789, and Storrs Hall, built for Sir John Legard, followed in 1790. Elleray, the home of Professor John Wilson from Paisley, was completed in 1808, while Silver Holme, Pull Woods, Ecclerigg House and The Briery all followed shortly afterwards.

Until the coming of the railways, Windermere was the almost

exclusive province of the upper middle classes, but the opening of the branch line from Oxenholme to Windermere in 1847 brought with it an entirely new clientele. Excursion trains from the industrial towns of South Lancashire soon began to disgorge their passengers at the newly created village of Windermere, situated in the township of Applethwaite over a mile from the water's edge. In almost no time at all, the growth of hotels, shops and boarding-houses sent the resident population of the township rocketing from 664 in 1851 to 2,252 in 1891. The first steam yacht, *Lady of the Lake*, appeared in 1845, while the opening of the Furness Railway's branch line to Lakeside in 1868 was followed by the launching of their screw-steamers *Swan* and *Tern*.

Windermere was not the only settlement to experience a phenomenal growth with the coming of the railways. Bowness, too, expanded rapidly in the 1870s, aided by the capital investment of H.W. Schneider, the Furness industrialist, who settled at Belsfield after the opening of the railway from Lakeside to Barrow. Ambleside, although it escaped the invasion of the railway in 1847, did not withstand the influx of hotels and lodging-houses and grew steadily outwards towards the steamer pier at Waterhead from 1850 onwards. Only the smaller villages and hamlets of the more inaccessible western shore escaped the mushroom growth of the late Victorian era, and even today the Sawreys and Hawkshead are relatively quiet backwaters when compared with the bustling activity surrounding the promenade at Bowness Bay or at Waterhead.

With the coming of the motor car in the twentieth century, the tourist industy has experienced an even greater explosive growth. Windermere, today, is undoubtedly one of the most attractive spots in the British Isles, and each year hundreds of thousands of visitors flock to enjoy its beauty. But it is this overwhelming popularity which itself threatens to destroy the very beauty and tranquillity that the urban dweller seeks. Indeed, it was as a result of the British Government's firm commitment to preserve a number of outstanding areas of largely unspoilt countryside that in 1951 the Lake District was designated one of the country's first national parks.

In an age of active environmental lobbies and rigorous

planning controls aimed at protecting the landscape from the hand of man, it is salutary, however, to remember that the outstanding beauty of the Windermere area is not as natural as appears at first sight. From the establishment of the first Neolithic settlement right up to the present day, countless generations have been repeatedly changing and moulding the landscape of the Windermere area; and they will no doubt continue to do so in the future. It is the responsibility of the planners – and of all those who love the area – to ensure that, while the landscape will inevitably be altered, it must never be spoiled.

And while it is clear that the Windermere landscape will always bear the stamp of man, it is equally true that the landscape has retained a strong, distinctive natural beauty of its own. Indeed, it is a landscape which could not have been adapted to its present form by man had not the immense forces of nature carved the rocks into shape during the innumerable centuries before man ever settled in this area.

2

Exploring the Windermere Landscape

Anyone who visits Bowness Bay on a busy bank holiday, or drives bumper-to-bumper on the road through Ambleside, could be forgiven for suggesting that the Windermere area is overcrowded during the holiday season. Yet this superficial impression reveals only a small part of the true picture, and such an opinion can only be justified by one who has neither sufficient time nor the inclination to explore the area more fully. Certainly there are bottlenecks at the busiest times on some of the main roads, and the majority of day-trippers do tend to congregate at just a handful of popular sites on the lake shore. Another easily recognizable cause for concern is congestion on the lake itself, where the Windermere Recreation Survey of 1977 pointed to some of the dangers which could well result from its over-use.

Yet, if you are prepared to forget the most popular areas at the busiest times and to walk for even just a short distance, you can quickly get away from the noise and the bustle of the crowds and enjoy the peace and the quiet beauty of the Windermere landscape. Abandon the holiday-makers thronging the promenade at Bowness, and within half an hour you can be sitting alone on a rocky knoll, looking down at the tiny ants bustling backwards and forwards along the foreshore. Or park the car at Waterhead and cross the fields which rise up behind the Ghyll Head Hotel, and within minutes you can be lost to the world in the woodlands overlooking Windermere or perched on Jenkyn's Crag looking out along the whole length of the lake. Or take a picnic lunch and while away the hours ambling alongside the many charming little tarns dotted across the summit of

Claife Heights, where you will be unlikely to see more than a handful of people all day.

With an abundance of public footpaths in the Windermere area, there are many trails and paths which have been waymarked to help visitors explore the district more closely on foot. These vary in length from the short nature walks laid out by the National Trust on the Claife Shore of Windermere and at White Moss Common, to the six-mile waymarked footpath across Claife Heights between the Ferry and Hawkshead, opened by HRH the Duke of Edinburgh in 1966. In Grizedale Forest, visitors can either follow the short Mill Beck Forest Trail or attempt the $9\frac{1}{2}$-mile track along the Silurian Way – a long-distance footpath created by the Forestry Commission to link the peaks overlooking the Grizedale valley.

Wherever you choose to walk, your journey will be enriched if you set out with something of the spirit of exploration. The landscape still holds many secrets from the past, and anyone who takes the time to search closely may well discover features that other people have simply overlooked. The true explorer does not rush from A to B hoping to cover as much ground as possible in the minimum of time; instead he allows plenty of time to observe the small-scale features and to ponder on their significance. He enjoys the fine views and the beautiful scenery, but he does not ignore the more humble and commonplace objects round about him. Many of the features we observe in the landscape are much older than we may imagine at first sight, and most of the items we take for granted – such as stone walls, farm buildings, trees and streams – have an interesting story to tell if only we pause and take a second look.

The Windermere landscape has much to reveal if only we try to unravel its message. We may, for example, observe an old channel leading from a stream bed. Immediately this raises several questions. Where does it convey the water to? Can we find the remains of an ancient mill? What was the mill used for? Why was it sited here? Which local raw materials did it use? A simple observation such as this can set off a whole chain of questions for which we can then start to look for answers. If we explore in this way, the landscape will soon start to speak to us of the past.

Perhaps the best place to start exploring the area is in the village of Windermere itself. It is near here that most visitors catch their first glimpse of the lake, and in this Victorian settlement the growth of tourism in the nineteenth century has had its most obvious effect on the landscape. From the entrance to Windermere Station it is quite easy to picture the route that the Kendal and Windermere Railway would have followed had it ever been extended across the main road and along St Catherine's Walk towards Low Wood or Ambleside. But it is far more difficult to imagine what the scene must have looked like before the railway arrived. If we walk down the hill towards the main shopping area, it is hard to realize that not one of the buildings around us stood here before the railway was opened in 1847. Yet, if we look more closely, it is clear that the pointed towers and the mock-Gothic frontages reflect the self-confidence and grandeur of the Victorian era. It can be interesting to spend a few minutes searching for date-stones on the buildings and attempting to discover which were the first buildings to be erected in the village. A small terraced cottage in Cross Street bears the date 1858, only eleven years after the railway was built, and a gable end with the date 1859 can be found nearby on Victoria Street. But are these really the oldest dwellings in the town?

Generally speaking, the nearer the station, the older the buildings, and certainly the grandest of all the Victorian buildings is found just above the station on the opposite side of the main road. The Windermere Hotel was built by Richard Rigg to coincide with the opening of the Kendal and Windermere Railway. The scale of the building shows the confidence with which the family celebrated the coming of the railway. The Rigg family operated stage-coaches throughout the southern part of the Lake District, but, far from seeing the railway as a threat, they welcomed the new trade that the railway would bring and laid on connecting coach services to Hawkshead, Ambleside, Keswick and beyond.

If we follow the path opposite the station, signposted to Orrest Head, we can very shortly look down upon the rear of the Windermere Hotel and see the great extent of the stables, where once dozens of horses were kept. How different Windermere must have been when the roar of cars was absent, and the pace of life was much slower than at present. Today the quiet path winding up between the rhododendrons and laurel bushes provides an immediate respite from the noise of the traffic rushing past on the main road. Yet there have been plans to build a bypass through these pleasant woodlands, and should such a scheme ever come to fruition, the peace and quiet along this charming approach to Orrest Head would be shattered for ever.

As we pass through a kissing-gate and leave the woodlands behind, we are reminded by a plaque that Orrest Head – like so many of the local beauty spots – is in the care of the National Trust. This land is, indeed, one of the earliest acquisitions of the Trust, having been presented in memory of Arthur Henry Heywood of Elleray in 1902. A final climb to the summit reveals a superb view both up and down the lake. In the distance Loughrigg Fell rises beyond the northern reach of Windermere, while the characteristic pointed peaks of the Langdale Pikes are easy to recognize towering above the valley of Langdale. Beyond the Troutbeck valley, the sloping fields of the Troutbeck Hundreds rise up almost to the summit of Wansfell Pike, while to the south of the valley, capping the ridge beyond Far Orrest Farm, lies the rocky knoll of Allen Knott, whose summit is surmounted by the ramparts of an Iron Age hill fort. Looking across the lake beyond Belle Grange on a clear day, the slopes of Coniston Old Man and Wetherlam dominate the western skyline, while to the north of the Wrynose Pass, the summit of Scafell Pike – the highest peak in England – can just be seen peeping out from behind the ridge of Bowfell. To the south the glistening lake bed snakes away towards Gummer's How and the lower fells around Newby Bridge. At a single glance, the impact of the major geological formations can be picked out quite easily. Northwards lie the high, jagged peaks which have been carved out of the resistant rocks of the Borrowdale Volcanic Series, while to the south the gentler and more rounded summits are typical of the lower and less resistant Silurian hill country.

If we leave the summit of Orrest Head by a distinct grassy track to the north, the bracken and rough grassland of the summit are soon replaced on the lower slopes by improved pasture. When Thomas West wrote his *Guide to The Lakes* in 1778, he observed that the slopes of Orrest Head were already divided into small enclosures, and the fellside was cultivated right up to the summit. The lower land around Orrest Head was once common land, part of Applethwaite Common, but was enclosed by an Act of Parliament of 1831. Before the slump in corn prices during the nineteenth century, much of this land was ploughed up for grain crops. Today, however, the land is used entirely for pasture, and Causeway Farm at the foot of the hill has all the characteristic features of a modern dairy farm, including slurrystore, silage pit, cattle stalls and milking parlour. Before crossing Wynlass Beck on a small stone slab bridge, the footpath crosses the line of the aqueduct from Windermere to Kendal. Nature has quickly healed the scars wrought by man, and only a very observant visitor would notice the inspection chamber in the field to the west of the footpath. Here, at least, there can be no claim that the water abstraction scheme has caused any permanent damage to the landscape.

Beyond the gate, the walled lane which leads past the farm may well follow the route trod by Roman soldiers marching from their camp at Alavna, south of Kendal, to the fort at Galava, near the head of the lake. The name of the farm – 'Causeway' – certainly suggests the proximity of an ancient routeway, and the Roman road almost certainly followed the low-lying land between Banner Rigg and Capple Howe. The present winding track is certainly a very old-established routeway and constituted the only direct link between Kendal and Ambleside before the present line of the main road passing through Windermere village was adopted. Beyond an area of mixed woodland, the road passes close beside a farm bearing the name 'Crosses'. While the architecture of the building and a prominent date plaque suggests that the house was built as part of a local estate in 1897, the original settlement is in fact much earlier, and the name 'Crosshouse' is recorded at this site as early as 1558. Could the name refer to a wayside preaching cross erected beside this ancient trackway by an early Celtic saint? Or does it relate to the medieval chapel built in honour of St Catherine which was erected on the roadside just near here?

Beyond Crosses, the road winds down to St Catherine's, a

large mansion which was once the home of the Earl and Countess of Bradford. The old pack-horse route veers off to the right down St Catherine's Brow, descending steeply to the floor of the Troutbeck valley. The well by the roadside at the top of the brow must have been a welcome relief for travellers and their horses when they had just completed the steep climb up the brow from Troutbeck Bridge.

At the foot of the hill, a public footpath strikes across a field beyond a wrought-iron gateway, and this pleasant pathway leads across Wynlass Beck and through a woodland bedecked in the spring with wild daffodils. The stream once powered a busy cornmill which served the local township of Applethwaite, but today the only noise comes from the stream itself as it cascades over a series of falls and rapids before entering the lake at Low Millerground. A little further through the woodlands, the footpath crosses the driveway leading to Elleray, a modest Georgian mansion built in 1808 for Professor Wilson of Paisley. John Wilson, while still a student at Oxford, had inherited a fortune and purchased the Elleray estate. In 1807 he came to live in a small cottage on the estate while he planned and built his new mansion, deliberately sited to give a view up and down the whole length of the lake. In his *Recreations of Christopher North*, Wilson wrote, 'Windermere, seen by sunset from the spot where we now stand, Elleray, is at this moment the most beautiful scene on this earth.' The small cottage where Wilson first settled is now called Old Elleray and lies just to the north of the public footpath. Beyond here, the path follows the line of the proposed extension to the Windermere railway, and a cutting through the rock face, just before the footpath re-emerges near Windermere Station, was part of the preliminary work carried out by the railway company before the scheme was finally abandoned.

To the south of Windermere village, the settlement at Bowness bears a superficial resemblance to its larger neighbour. The elegance and flamboyance of Victorian architecture once again dominate the main streets, but a short walk in the area around the parish church quickly reveals evidence of buildings much older than those which can be found near Windermere Station. The New Hall Inn proudly boasts its connections with the local wrestler Thomas Longmire, who was landlord here from

1852 to 1860, while earlier records place the foundation of the hostelry at the beginning of the seventeenth century. Behind the parish church, the 'Stag's Head' still offers 'Post horses for hire', while St Martin's Church itself has a foundation dating back to at least 1328, when the new parish of Windermere was created.

Leaving the centre of Bowness, the road to Windermere village climbs steeply up Crag Brow. Once again, the dates of construction reveal a progression of building outwards along Lake Road towards the railway station, and while the shops on Crag Brow were constructed around 1860, those further along the road nearer The Craig bear later dates, such as 1873 and 1887. At the top of Crag Brow, where a large chestnut tree used to stand, Helm Road strides off up the hillside and provides a quick line of retreat from the bustling crowds on a busy day. A little way along Craig Walk can be found the delightful almshouses which were built by Henry Schneider when he was chairman of the local Board of Guardians, and adjacent to these are row upon row of elegant terraced houses built during the great expansion of Bowness at the end of the nineteenth century. Perched on a high rocky knoll, and looking out over the lake, sits the Windermere Hydropathic Hotel. The elegant frontage was constructed in 1881 when the fashion of 'taking the waters' was at its height. Today tastes have changed, but the hotel still retains its magnificent view across Bowness Bay.

Beyond the Windermere Hydro, Helm Road climbs steeply up to the rocky precipice of Biskey Howe. The energetic may follow a small, steep path leading through the woods to the summit, but the road itself climbs nearly all the way, and a gently sloping footpath for wheelchairs leads from the roadside for the benefit of disabled visitors. From the rugged crags on the summit of Biskey Howe there is an excellent view over Bowness Bay and northwards across the lake towards Ambleside. This was a popular spot with early visitors, and a few moments' search will reveal the well-worn steps cut into the solid rock to enable the ladies of the party to gain the summit of the outcrop in the most graceful manner. Today the distant peaks can be identified on a view indicator erected to commemorate Queen Elizabeth II's Silver Jubilee in 1977.

If we re-trace our steps to the road and proceed along the

public footpath through an old gateway marked 'Private', we shortly reach a wicket gate leading into the National Trust property of Post Knott. This wide footpath, with its carefully engineered gradient, was another favourite perambulation of the Victorians. The footpath was deliberately constructed to provide easy access to the summit of Post Knott, and stone seats were built into the wall at regular intervals to enable visitors to sit and enjoy the view. Near the summit of the hill, the original path steepens for a few yards and swings round to the left, where an observation platform was levelled to provide a viewpoint up and down the lake. Today the trees have grown up to such an extent that – especially in the summer – they all but obscure the view, but a better panorama is revealed on the open, rocky land to the south, which is easily accessible through a wicket gate.

From Post Knott we can look down on Bowness Bay, some three hundred feet below, and observe the tiny figures milling backwards and forwards along the promenade. The area adjacent to the Victorian bandstand, known as 'the Glebe', once formed part of the arable fields belonging to the rector and was worked by the villagers as part of their service due to the church. On the enclosure of Undermillbeck Common in 1822, the common lands of the township were divided up amongst the major landholders, and the Glebe Farm, adjacent to the rectory, became a smaller and self-contained unit, which it remains to this day. Post Knott provides an excellent view across the lake to Claife Heights and down the southern reaches of the lake beyond the Ferry. From Ferry Nab, the old pack-horse route to Kendal climbed steeply up Longtail Hill and across the flank of Post Knott before making its way across Undermillbeck Common to Kendal. Before the coming of the railway, the post-boy would ride along this road from Kendal and upon approaching the Knott would blow his post horn to warn the inhabitants of Bowness of his impending arrival.

To the south of the rocky summit, a winding path descends steeply to the Kendal road. In places this footpath follows the original well-graded Victorian path; elsewhere a keen eye can make out the terraces where the earlier path has been abandoned in favour of the shorter, and steeper, modern track. Following the Kendal road back to the centre of Bowness, we pass the main entrance to the Belsfield Hotel, formerly the private residence of H.W. Schneider. A little further along the road we pass Laurel Cottage, which housed the original Windermere Grammar School founded in 1613, before once again reaching the centre of the village.

To the south of Bowness, the main road to Newby Bridge soon crosses the Black Beck, the old boundary between Westmorland and Lancashire. This old frontier – still marked by a boundary stone – came into existence during Norman times and separated the newly created Barony of Kendal from the lands of William Marshall, Earl of Pembroke. The boundary follows the course of the stream for some distance from the shores of Windermere and is then picked up along the line of an ancient boundary bank near Winster village. To the south of the boundary, the lands of Cartmel Fell passed into the hands of Cartmel Priory in 1188, and it was the tenants of the priory who first reclaimed large areas of the fell for agriculture.

The narrow Fell Road leads off the main road at Gill Head, a magnificent yeoman farmer's house built in 1719. A few yards further on, a public footpath signed 'Rosthwaite' branches left along a driveway before crossing a stile beside a plantation of Norway spruce and Scots pine. Beyond the next gate, the trackway strides off across Rosthwaite Allotment. During the time of the priory, tenants were allowed to fence only small portions of the land, and most of Cartmel Fell was held as common grazing land. The demise of the priory in 1536 saw the enlargement of these smallholdings and the creation of enclosed pastures. This process was carried to its logical extension by the formal enclosure of Cartmel Fell by an Act of Parliament of 1796. The common land was divided into small units, and allotments were made to existing tenants who held rights of common pasture. Rosthwaite Allotment, based on the farmstead of Rosthwaite, was one of these, and today sheep and cattle still graze the heathery slopes and the grassy knolls of Rosthwaite Heights. The farmhouse itself dates back to the seventeenth century, though modern alterations and extensions show that hill farming in this area is still very much a viable occupation. Beyond the duck pond, a path leads over a stile and up through a plantation of mature larch trees. In common with many of the steeper slopes on the fell, the area was afforested in the early nineteenth century, following the enclosure of the commons.

From the summit of Rulbuts Hill, an extensive view opens up across the Winster valley to the south and east. In the foreground, the pleasant meadows of the Winster valley would have been flooded by a huge reservoir had plans submitted by Manchester Corporation Water Works been approved during the 1960s. Beyond the valley, the edge of a geological fault is marked by the white Carboniferous Limestone cliffs of Whitbarrow Scar, while in the distance the rounded summits of the Howgill Fells and the Central Pennines are visible on a clear day. At the mouth of the valley, the River Winster drains into Morecambe Bay, and during the higher sea levels immediately following the Ice Age a huge arm of the sea must have extended all the way inland as far as Winster village.

Descending towards the Winster valley, the path soon meets a more distinct cart track climbing southwards across the broken land. This track follows the path of one of the original enclosure roads laid out systematically by the Enclosure Commissioners to link the newly enclosed pastures with the existing farmsteads and hamlets. Today these roads are often little more than cart tracks, enclosed by stone walls erected as new boundaries at the end of the eighteenth century. One of these narrow enclosure roads leads up from Birket Houses to Birket Houses Allotment, and from here a footpath crosses the fell back to Ghyll Head. This area of the fell has almost completely reverted to how it must have looked before the enclosure took place. Much of the land between the rocky knolls is poorly drained grassland, and large areas are covered in bracken and gorse, with a few stunted silver birch trees reminding us of the former tree cover. The footpath rejoins the Ghyll Head Road near Rowan Tree Tarn, a small local reservoir, where nearby the National Park Authority has purchased a small area of public access land for the enjoyment of the public.

At the foot of the lake much of the land is now in the ownership of the Forestry Commission. Although based in the Grizedale valley, outliers of the Grizedale Forest extend well beyond the western shores of Windermere in the vicinity of Staveley-in-Cartmel. Changes in policy have ensured that members of the public are no longer prohibited from these state-owned forests, and walkers are welcome to explore the forests on the elaborate network of forest roads and tracks. On the old turnpike road between Newby Bridge, Crosthwaite and Kendal, the Forestry Commission have laid out a car-park and picnic area at Astley's Plantation, conveniently situated near the footpath to Gummer's How.

From the rocky promontory beyond the stile, one has an almost aerial view across the southern reaches of the lake. Directly opposite, the lake steamers tie up alongside the extensive quay which was built for the opening of the Furness Railway's Lakeside Branch in 1868. Today steam trains once again provide a connecting service with the lake steamers, leaving Lakeside for a four-mile nostalgic journey down the Backbarrow Gorge to Haverthwaite. The gorge was formed by glacial meltwaters overflowing from the Windermere valley, and from Gummer's How it is easy to appreciate how deeply the river has cut down though the former watershed. To the south the former valley floor, masked by hummocky morainic deposits, stretches towards Cartmel and Cark, and stages in the retreat of the ice from the Windermere valley are marked by ridges of terminal moraine which are just visible at the southern end of the lake, beyond the first loop of the river. On the opposite bank the high ice-marginal channel at Finsthwaite, once followed by a spur of ice, has now clearly been left as an abandoned valley, lying some two hundred feet above the floor of the main trough.

Nestling in the main valley floor lies the little village of Staveley-in-Cartmel, with its charming little church dedicated to St Mary. A chapel was first built on this site shortly after the dissolution of Cartmel Priory in 1536, but the church is not mentioned in any documents until 1618, when Henry Longman was recorded as the first incumbent. The church has been restored on several occasions, and the tower was erected in 1793. The graveyard dates only from 1841, but even in such a relatively recent burial ground a quick survey of the headstones reveals some interesting local names such as 'Ashburner', full of significance and meaning.

Between the Backbarrow Gorge and the Finsthwaite valley rises the isolated summit of Finsthwaite Heights. At one time this hill was regarded as a popular 'station' from which extensive views could be gained across the lake, and a wide, well-graded footpath leads to the summit from the northern side. Today, however, the summit is more easily reached by a footpath from Newby Bridge. Before the building of the main road along the side of the Backbarrow Gorge, the bridge at Newby Bridge was a vital link in the route of the turnpike road from Kendal to Dalton. A little way downstream from the bridge lies the weir which maintains the level of the water in Windermere at approximately 129 feet above sea level.

Beyond the railway bridge, opposite a row of cottages constructed by the Furness Railway Company, a track leads off towards Finsthwaite, and, beyond a stile, a footpath quickly climbs to the summit through a mixed woodland of Scots pine, holly, yew and silver birch. On the top of Finsthwaite Heights are the remains of a tower erected in 1799, 'To Honour the Officers, Seamen and Marines of the Royal Navy whose matchless Conduct, and irresistible Valour, decisively defeated the Fleets of France, Spain and Holland and preserved and protected LIBERTY and COMMERCE.' The door is now bricked up, and the tower is unused, but in its day it provided an excellent viewpoint across the southern reaches of the lake, and southwards towards the Leven Estuary and Morecambe Bay.

From the tower a footpath leads down through a silver birch plantation into the Finsthwaite valley, from where a public footpath leads across open fields to Finsthwaite. The village contains a number of interesting and ancient buildings, including Bullace Cottage, dating from 1608. The church, however, is quite out of character with the local architecture and is relatively modern. It was erected in 1874 when the simple lines of the older chapel were replaced in a characteristic act of Victorian vandalism. At the same time, a new village school was erected near the church, and its recent closure is a more modern testimony to the decline of village life in the Lake District.

A short walk along the road through the village leads to the Stott Park bobbin mill, which has recently been renovated to its former working condition by the Department of the Environment. The lathes used for shaping the bobbins were operated by a thirty-two-foot-high breast wheel, which was powered by water led down the hillside from an artificial lake. The course of the leat and the underground pipes can still be traced today with a little detective work and imagination. Behind the upper car-park, the road was formerly spanned by a wooden trough which carried the water across to the wheelhouse. In the woodlands beyond, the path of the leat ran along the contour while, a little further along the road towards Finsthwaite, the line of the underground channel can be followed by the ceramic pipes of the ventilation shafts which penetrate the surface in the woodlands alongside the road. Near the entrance to High Dam car-park, a small weir in the stream bed and an iron grille at the base of the wall indicate the point where the water was led off into the leat, flowing underneath the road before entering the enclosed pipeline system which led down to the bobbin mill.

From the High Dam car-park, a public footpath follows the beck upstream, climbing steadily through a mixed woodland of silver birch and larch. Beyond a wicket gate, the path first reaches the small man-made tarn at Low Dam, with its attractively wooded banks, before leading on to the much larger High Dam. The woodlands surrounding High and Low Dam have been opened to the public by the National Park Authority, and the area has rapidly become a popular venue for family picnics.

Much of the shore of Windermere itself is today under private ownership, and public access to the lakeside is severely restricted, especially on the western bank of the lake in the area south of Cunsey Beck. North of the Ferry, however, the foreshore has come under the guardianship of the National Trust, and the public are allowed free access to almost the whole stretch of the lake side between the Ferry and Wray Castle. There are many interesting walks in the woodlands overlooking the lake, and it is well worth exploring the woods and tarns of Claife Heights.

From the Ferry House, which now serves as the laboratories of the Freshwater Biological Association, the road to Hawkshead winds its way uphill through Far Sawrey village and along to Near Sawrey. Here, by the roadside, is Hill Top, the seventeenth-century farmhouse which became the home of Beatrix Potter and which is featured in many of the illustrations in her children's books. The house, which is furnished with many of the author's personal possessions, is now owned by the National Trust and is open to the public. Nearby is the 'Tower Bank Arms', featured in the illustrations to *The Story of Jemima Puddleduck* and also owned by the National Trust.

Beyond Castle Farm, a bridleway leads gradually uphill to the gently rolling summit of Claife Heights. The pathway is flanked by dry-stone walls dating from the enclosure of the common lands following the Act of Parliament of 1794. Many of the resulting fields are of approximately ten acres – the acreage considered by the agricultural reformers of the day to be the most efficient size for controlled grazing. On the higher land, the enclosures are often much larger than this, indicating the much more ancient intake land which was wrested from the waste by the yeoman farmers who were direct descendants of the tenants of Furness Abbey.

After being joined by another trackway coming direct from Far Sawrey, the bridlepath soon passes beside Moss Eccles Tarn, a delightful spot where Beatrix Potter used to relax with her small wooden rowing-boat. The boat was subsequently recovered from the bed of the lake and is now on display at the Windermere Steamboat Museum. A little way beyond Moss Eccles Tarn, another footpath bears off to the right and leads towards Three Dubs Tarn, a smaller lake completely surrounded by woodland and furnished with a small boathouse dated 1908. This date gives us a clue as to when the tarn was constructed, for all the delightful small tarns on Claife Heights are actually man-made, and none of them appears on the early Ordnance Survey maps of the nineteenth century. Three Dubs Tarn is in fact a small reservoir, built for storing water in an age when water-power was still used as an efficient form of energy, and sections of the pipe carrying water away from the Tarn can be discovered running overground towards the south.

Two footpaths join at Three Dubs, and if the second path is followed through the plantation, it eventually joins the old track leading from Belle Grange to Far Sawrey. Once again we walk alongside fields which were created by enclosure at the end of the eighteenth century. It was here that John Christian Curwen carried out his agricultural reforms, breeding Dairy Shorthorn cattle and experimenting with new crop rotations. Following the footpath signed to the Ferry, we begin to descend the steep slopes which were planted with thousands of larches by John Curwen in the years after 1799.

As we approach the Ferry, we pass beneath the ruined arch of an old dilapidated building. This is all that remains of the summerhouse built at West's 'First Station' for visitors to catch their first glimpse of Windermere. Today the walls are in ruins, and the trees have grown to such a height that one would have great difficulty in seeing the lake, even if the building was intact. A short way beyond 'The Station', the footpath rejoins the main road near Ferry House.

With the extensive afforestation of Claife Heights during the eighteenth and nineteenth centuries, there are now few places on the summit of the Heights where a clear view can be gained across to the eastern shores of the lake. One of these points is the triangulation pillar at High Blind How, on the waymarked footpath between Hawkshead and the Ferry. Here a rocky knoll has been deliberately cleared so that walkers can look down across the middle reaches of Windermere and gain a bird's-eye view of Bowness beyond. Another excellent viewpoint is Latterbarrow, the only individual summit to rise well above the plateau-like surface of Claife Heights, and the only one to have been left completely unplanted.

Latterbarrow can be approached either along the waymarked forest trail – from the Ferry or from Colthouse – or by a number of paths leading from Hawkshead village. Starting from the car-park at Hawkshead, one is almost bound to pass the red sandstone grammar school building where Wordsworth studied from 1778 to 1783 before going up to Cambridge and where he carved his name for posterity on one of the wooden desks. From outside the grammar school, the way in which the parish church dominates the settlement is quite clear. Built on a high mound of glacial boulder clay, the original church was deliberately sited by the monks of Furness Abbey to act as a focal point for the community. The market, held in the largest of the squares, only became the focal point of the settlement after the dissolution of the abbey. Today the market hall remains as a testimony to the once-flourishing trade of the village, but, with the decline of the local woollen trade during the nineteenth century, the market collapsed and the settlement never grew to the size of a town. Walking northwards out of the village, it is easy to see that the settlement has hardly expanded beyond its medieval boundaries, and within two or three hundred yards of the market-place the road is lined on either side by fields.

To the north of the village lies the gatehouse of Hawkshead Hall, all that remains of the former mansion of the abbots of Furness. The manorial court of the abbey was held in a room overlooking the gateway, and this part of the old hall is now open as a museum under the auspices of the National Trust. To the north of the courthouse, a quiet by-way, lined with upturned slates used for fencing, leads across the valley to the Colthouse – Wray road. Looking out across the flat valley floor, it is easy to realize that Esthwaite Water must, at one time, have reached all the way up to this point, and the valley floor has been infilled by river sediments only since the end of the Ice Age.

Beyond the junction with the Colthouse road, a rocky footpath winds up the hillside in the direction of Latterbarrow. Before reaching the spruce and larch plantations on Renny Crags, the path climbs steeply to the summit, which is surmounted by a well-built monumental cairn, known as 'Latterbarrow Man'. From the top of the fell there is a clear view in all directions, stretching from Coniston Old Man, Bowfell and the Langdale Pikes across to Fairfield, Dollywaggon Pike and the Ill Bell range overlooking Kentmere. A better view of Windermere itself is revealed if one walks some fifty yards to the east of the cairn, and from here the whole of the northern reach of the lake, from Waterhead to White Cross Bay, comes clearly into view.

Of all the centres from which to explore the Windermere area, Ambleside is probably the most spectacular. Perhaps this is because, of all the villages surrounding Windermere, only Ambleside is situated on the Borrowdale Volcanic rocks and is therefore the only settlement to be surrounded by the rugged angular peaks typical of the Central Lake District. One can get the 'feel' of this central mountainous region, without climbing too high, if one ascends the slopes of Loughrigg Fell – especially when taking the short, steep path from the bridge at Clappersgate up to the summit of Todd Crag. The jagged, angular nature of the volcanic rocks is quickly evident, and the steepness of the climb contrasts sharply with the gentle walks on the rolling Silurian foothills to the south.

From the rocky summit of Todd Crag one can look south across the northern reaches of Windermere as far as Bowness Bay. Beyond Brathay Bridge lie Old Brathay and Brathay Hall, now the headquarters of the Brathay Exploration Group, while nearer the mouth of the Rothay, beyond the Brathay confluence, one has an 'aerial' view of the remains of the Roman camp at Galava. To the east a marvellous panoramic view opens up across Ambleside, and one can easily trace the development of the settlement from its early stages to the present time. To the north of Stock Beck, the square tower of St Anne's Hall marks the site of the early parish church and the nucleus of the ancient settlement 'above Stock'. At the foot of Peggy Hill, Braithwaite's cornmill and the old bark mill can be seen straddling the beck on either side of 'Rattle Gill'. Beyond the Bridge House and the main Keswick road lie Braithwaite Fold and the site of the old Ambleside Hall. 'Below Stock' are the sprawling Victorian suburbs, reaching out towards the steamer pier at Waterhead and marching across the floor of the Rothay valley towards Loughrigg itself. The dominant landmark in this quarter of the town is the round spire of St Mary's parish church, built by Sir George Gilbert Scott in 1854 and symbolizing the confidence and brashness of the Victorian era. Behind the town, Scandale Fell and Wansfell Pike rise steeply from the valley floor, while in the distance the jagged, angular peaks of Ill Bell and Yoke are characteristic of the effect of glacial erosion on the resistant volcanic rocks.

Leaving the summit of Loughrigg Fell in the direction of Ambleside, the path descends steeply through light woodland before meeting a cart track near Brow Head Farm, where two former barns have been most attractively converted into houses. At the foot of the hill – not far from Fox How, once the home of Dr Arnold of Rugby – a path leads over Miller Bridge and across Rothay Park to the parish church. Beyond the church, the Victorian suburbs were built in the tide of rising prosperity follow the opening of the Kendal and Windermere Railway in 1847. Compston Road was laid out as a main thoroughfare in 1906, while Millans Park was developed as a wealthy middle-class suburb during the 1890s. Beyond the bus station – laid out on the site of the former tenter fields – lies the older nucleus of Ambleside-below-Stock. The Queen's Hotel and the Salutation Inn (dating from 1656) are two of the oldest hostelries in the town, while the market hall (1863) and the Mechanics' Institute (1858) were built on the site of the old market-place.

Beyond Cheapside, behind the market hall, a road winds up the hillside to Stock Ghyll Park, where a footpath climbs alongside Stock Beck. In previous centuries Stock Beck powered a whole succession of mills as it twisted and tumbled down the hillside. Today the machinery is quiet, but the remains of weirs, leats, tailraces – and sometimes the mills themselves – can still be seen. One of the best sites – and probably one of the earliest – is here at Stock Ghyll Park, where a weir, still intact, carried water to a nineteenth-century bobbin mill, situated on the opposite bank. The waterwheel operated a series of lathes, which shaped the bobbins before despatch to the Lancashire cotton mills. Little remains of the original machinery, but the tailrace is still clearly visible some distance downstream from the weir, and the coppice sheds which were once used to store the timber have been converted into holiday flatlets. Horrax's bobbin mill was not the first mill on this site, however, and during the seventeenth century water from this weir turned the wheel of an old corn mill. Immediately upstream is the site of a medieval fulling mill, which operated during the fifteenth century.

Stock Beck provided an excellent site for a number of watermills because of the steep gradient as it descends in a series of falls and rapids to the floor of the Windermere valley. It is an excellent example of a 'hanging valley' which tumbles over the edge of a steep-sided glacial trough. Nowhere is this more evident than a little further upstream, where at Stock Ghyll Force the water plunges over seventy feet in two main steps before resuming its helter-skelter course through the gorge to the valley below. A footbridge spans the stream above the falls, and a path rejoins the road through an old turnstile gate. From here one can climb to the summit of Wansfell Pike, or, walking downhill past the old grammar school buildings (now an annexe for Charlotte Mason College), one can follow the path across the fields towards Waterhead.

Waterhead, like Windermere village, is almost entirely the creation of the Railway Age. With the opening of the Furness Railway Company's branch line to Lakeside in 1868, large pleasure-steamers began plying up and down the lake between the newly constructed railhead at Lakeside, and the bustling waterhead only a mile distant from Ambleside. Not only did Ambleside begin to expand in the direction of the lake, but large houses and luxurious hotels were built only yards away from the landing stage. A contemporary writer described Waterhead as 'a sort of "Clapham Junction" of Lakeland', with steamers discharging passengers from the Furness Railway at Lakeside and stage-coaches conveying passengers from the rival company's terminus at Windermere.

Across the main road from the steamer pier, a narrow footpath climbs up the hillside between the Romney Hotel and the Ghyll Head Hotel. After crossing a field, the path climbs gently through a mixed deciduous woodland before meeting a track coming up from Ambleside. The track continues to climb in a series of zigzags, crossing a small beck before reaching the signpost for 'Jenkyn's Crag'. The crag itself is just a few yards from the track and provides an excellent view across the lake towards Blelham Tarn and Latterbarrow and down the northern reaches of the lake as far as Belle Isle. After taking in the peace and tranquillity of this delightful spot, the return to Waterhead can be made by retracing one's steps to the footbridge and then keeping to the footpath which leads down the southern side of the beck. This path winds down the hillside past Stagshaw Gardens, a National Trust property famous for its rhododendrons and azaleas. Alternatively, the track beyond Jenkyn's Crag provides an attractive walk through Skelghyll Woods and on to Troutbeck village.

Troutbeck itself is a fascinating little village, strung out for a mile and a half along the hillside and linked together by an intricate network of roads, tracks and footpaths – *all* worth exploring. Here there are many questions to be asked and many answers to be found. Why are the farms strung out along one road? Why were so many of the farmhouses built during the seventeenth century? Why are the parish church and the village school apparently so distant from the village? And why does the main road to Ullswater completely bypass the settlement? Some of the answers may be deduced on a visit to Town End, once the home of a local yeoman farmer, if one begins to understand the type of farming practised during the seventeenth century and its needs in terms of land. A walk along one of the many footpaths leading to Jesus Chapel may well reveal that the church was indeed far more central on foot than it is by car. And the wide, straight stretch of road between Limefitt Park and the Queen's Head should leave one in no doubt as to why it does not appear on the 1865 Ordnance Survey map.

Starting from Town Head, one can profitably combine an exploration of the northern part of the village with a walk to the summit of Wansfell Pike. Just north of the Queen's Head – a fine seventeenth-century house with a converted spinning gallery – the old road leaves the main road and climbs up towards High Green. At the top of the hill, the first of a series of yeats leads up via a narrow walled lane onto the hillside pastures above. Below the road, a network of winding, walled tracks leads down among the farmsteads, past a quaint cottage bearing the date 1690 and passing close by a statesman's house with a delightful example of a seventeenth-century spinning gallery. The track then climbs alongside the Mortal Man Inn, built around a cottage dating from 1689, before rejoining the road.

At Lane Foot Farm, another seventeenth-century farmstead some two hundred yards along the road, a drove road known as Nanny Lane leads up the hillside between dry-stone walls. As the track climbs higher, one can turn and observe the typical two-storey barn below at Lane Foot, and the corbie-stepped gables of the old cottage on the opposite side of the road. Less pleasing to the eye is the stark openness of the camping site on the valley floor, and the old quarry remains, partly obscured by conifers, on the opposite side of the valley above the Garburn Road.

Nanny Lane climbs for a considerable distance, flanked on either side by the former common pastures of the Troutbeck Hundreds, enclosed by the Act of Parliament of 1831. After about a mile, a cairned footpath leads across an area of rough pasture and out onto the unenclosed fell, with Wansfell Pike now clearly visible ahead. As the path climbs through the rough grassland and rocky outcrops up the southern flank of the fell, the view southwards across Windermere begins to open up, and one begins to appreciate that, at 1,581 feet, Wansfell Pike is the highest peak immediately overlooking Windermere.

Wansfell Pike has its feet firmly embedded in the tough, resistant volcanic rocks of the Borrowdale Volcanic Series, and it is directly as a result of this that it attains its dominant height. From the rocky outcrop on the summit the view is outstanding, and the contrast between the rugged volcanic peaks of the central mountainous core and the gently rolling Silurian foothills stands out clearly. To the north Froswick, Ill Bell, Yoke, Red Screes, Fairfield, the Langdale Pikes, Wetherlam and Old Man all belong to the Central Lake District. To the south, quite distinct but quite beautiful in their own right, lie the Silurian foothills – Claife Heights, Orrest Head, Brant Fell, Gummer's How. And between them lies Windermere, shining like a jewel in its deeply wooded trough, so far below us, yet so much the focus of our attention.

Even without the lake, the scenery would be superb. But with the longest lake in England stretched out before us, its calm, flat sheet complementing the rugged mountainsides, the Windermere landscape becomes quite magnificent. It is a landscape steeped in history; a landscape of great geographical variety and charm; a landscape bearing the stamp of man down the ages; a landscape which is well worth exploring.

3

Rocks, Rivers and Ice

Much of the individuality of the Windermere landscape is due to the inherent characteristics of the Silurian rocks which dominate the area. The sudden contrast between the gently rolling country of Southern Lakeland and the rugged, angular landforms of the Central Fells was no doubt noticed by the very earliest of travellers, but it was left to Jonathan Otley – the nineteenth-century watchmaker and amateur geologist from Keswick – to explain the differences. Over the years Otley had made a detailed study of the rocks of the Lake District, and he was the first to divide the region into three major rock types – the geological beds which are now referred to as the Skiddaw Slates, the Borrowdale Volcanics and the Silurian Slates. Otley initially set out his 'Remarks on the Succession of Rocks, in the District of the Lakes' in the *Lonsdale Magazine*, but his ideas gained a wider audience when he published a guide to the Lakes in 1823. His threefold division was adopted and developed by Adam Sedgwick, Professor of Geology at Cambridge, who in 1842 contributed three letters describing the rock types and their scenic effect to Wordsworth's *Complete Guide to the Lakes*. The geological history of the Lake District is complex, but even a brief outline of the sequence of geological events is sufficient to enable a visitor to understand the sharp contrasts of scenery in the Windermere area.

The oldest rocks in the Lake District are formed of mud and sand which were laid down on the floor of an extensive sea basin during Ordovician times, some 500 million years ago. In time, these sediments were folded and compressed into the series of dark grey shales and grits now known collectively as the Skiddaw Slates. Millions of years of erosion of these rocks were followed

Stock Ghyll Force, Ambleside

Gently rolling Silurian hill country at Gummer's How

Esthwaite Water

Applethwaite Common, from the rampart on the Iron Age hill fort at
Allen Knott

The Kentmere Range and Troutbeck Tongue

Remains of the Roman fort at Galava, near Waterhead

The fifteenth-century gatehouse at Hawkshead Hall served as a
courthouse for the abbots of Furness

Hawkshead parish church dominates the village

St Anthony's Chapel, Cartmel Fell, erected by the friars of Cartmel Priory

An ancient boundary bank near Winster

The Baptist chapel, Hawkshead Hill

A converted spinning gallery at the 'Queen's Head', Troutbeck

Town End, Troutbeck, home of the Browne family in the seventeenth century

Two-storey barn at Town End, with hay loft above and byre below

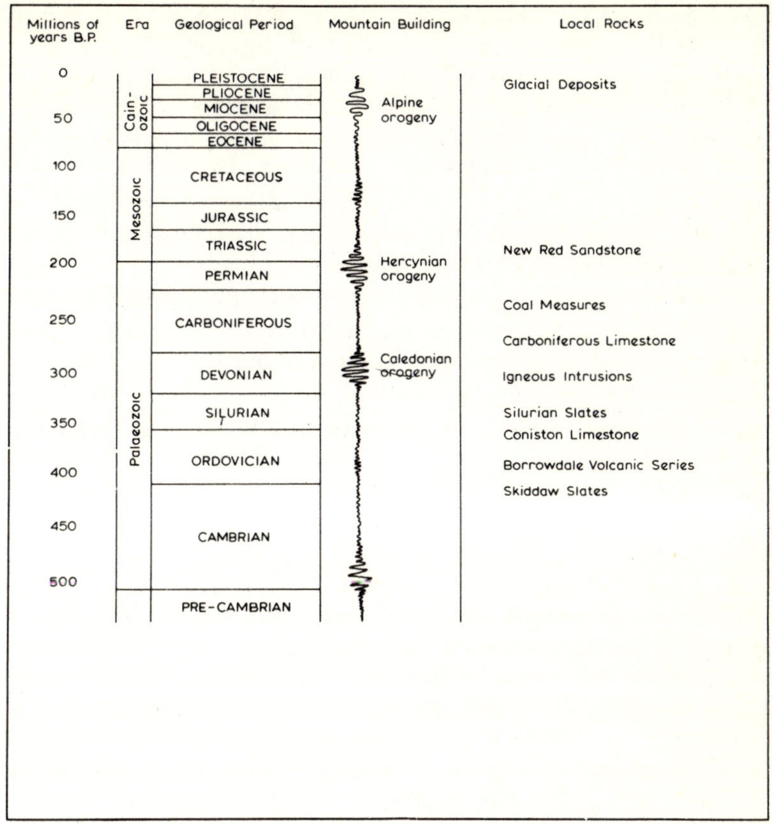

Geological column showing age of local rocks

by a rise in sea level, and it was on this Ordovician seabed that local volcanoes began to pour out their molten lava and ash, forming thousands of feet of andesite, tuff and other hard crystalline igneous rocks. Gradually this volcanic activity died down, and the green and grey rocks of the resulting Borrowdale Volcanic Series were folded and contorted by huge earth movements before being extensively eroded away by rivers and streams.

Towards the end of the Ordovician period, some 440 million years ago, the rising sea level once again flooded the area, causing a thin layer of calcareous mudstones and shelly limestones – the rocks of the Coniston Limestone Series – to be laid down on the bed of the shallow sea. This episode was followed by nearly 40 million years of marine sedimentation, during which rivers and streams deposited thousands of feet of mud and sand on the Silurian seabed. These dark bluey-grey mudstones and sandstones today form the Silurian Slates, an extensive series of shales and slates interspersed by coarse gritty sandstones and easily sheared flagstones.

The location at which each of these major rock type outcrops today is largely the result of extensive earth movements which have occurred since Silurian times. During the Devonian and Carboniferous periods, the rocks of the Lake District were repeatedly pushed up into a huge upfold, or anticline, thousands of feet high, while the resulting upland was subsequently eroded back down to sea level by rivers and streams. Newer sediments – including Carboniferous Limestone, Coal Measures and New Red Sandstone – were laid down on top of the older rocks but were each, in turn, eroded away from all but the fringes of the Lake District. During the Tertiary era which followed, the entire Lake District landmass was once again pushed upwards by earth movements, resulting in a huge dome-shaped massif. As in previous times, the youngest rocks at the centre of the dome were the first to be eroded away by rivers and streams, exposing the older rocks of the Borrowdale Volcanic Series and the Skiddaw Slates in the central part of the Lake District. The Skiddaw Slates – the most ancient rocks – outcrop to the north of Keswick, forming the smooth, resistant slopes of Skiddaw and Blencathra. To the south – and less extensively to the north – the high fells of Central Lakeland are chiselled out of the tough, resistant rocks of the Borrowdale Volcanic Series. These old, hard volcanic rocks stretch southwards as far as Ambleside, forming *en route* the craggy ridges of Helvellyn, Dollywaggon Pike and the Fairfield Horseshoe. To the north of Windermere, the slopes of Loughrigg Fell and Wansfell Pike bear the familiar rugged appearance of the resistant Borrowdale Volcanics. These are the rocks which form the *typical* Lakeland scenery of angular crags and steep rocky precipices – landforms characteristic of the central mountainous core into which Windermere extends only a fingertip at its northern end.

The boundary between these jagged mountains and the gentler rolling hillslopes of the younger Silurian Slates occurs less than a mile south of Ambleside, where the hard, crystalline greyey-green volcanic rocks give way to the less resistant bluey-grey shales of the Silurian beds. The change is marked by the belt of Coniston Limestone which crosses Windermere in a line running south of the River Brathay and Wansfell Pike. This narrow band of impure limestone outcrops again north of Troutbeck Church, from where it climbs diagonally across the slopes of Applethwaite Common in the vicinity of the Garburn Pass. The precise boundary is difficult to trace on the ground, but occasionally a local name – such as Limefitt Park in the Troutbeck valley, or Limestone Hill north of Hawkshead – indicates the site of a former lime-kiln located on the limestone of this narrow outcrop.

To the south of the Coniston Limestone belt, Windermere is bounded on all sides by the shales, grits, mudstones and flags of the Silurian series. These rocks are markedly less resistant than the volcanic rocks to the north and have been eroded more rapidly to form the lower and more gently rounded slopes of the Silurian foothills. The variety of rocks making up the Silurian Slates is illustrated to the north of Belle Grange where there is a complicated succession of mudstones and sandstones – the Stockdale Shales, Brathay Flags, Coldwell Beds and Coniston Grits – each bearing the name of the locality in which a notable outcrop of that particular rock type occurs. To the south, the greater part of the Windermere area is situated on the Bannisdale Slates, forming the characteristic bands of dark grey mudstone which outcrop repeatedly across the valley sides from the edge of the lake to the summits of Claife Heights and Gummer's How. These local variations in lithology have resulted in marked changes in relief as more resistant beds of rock have produced areas of higher land, while wide bays have been excavated where more easily eroded rocks occur on the lake shores. Gummer's How – the highest fell in the Silurian country – attains its outstanding stature only because it is composed of a somewhat harder band of gritstone within the Bannisdale Slates. In contrast, the deeply indented bay of Pull Wyke at the

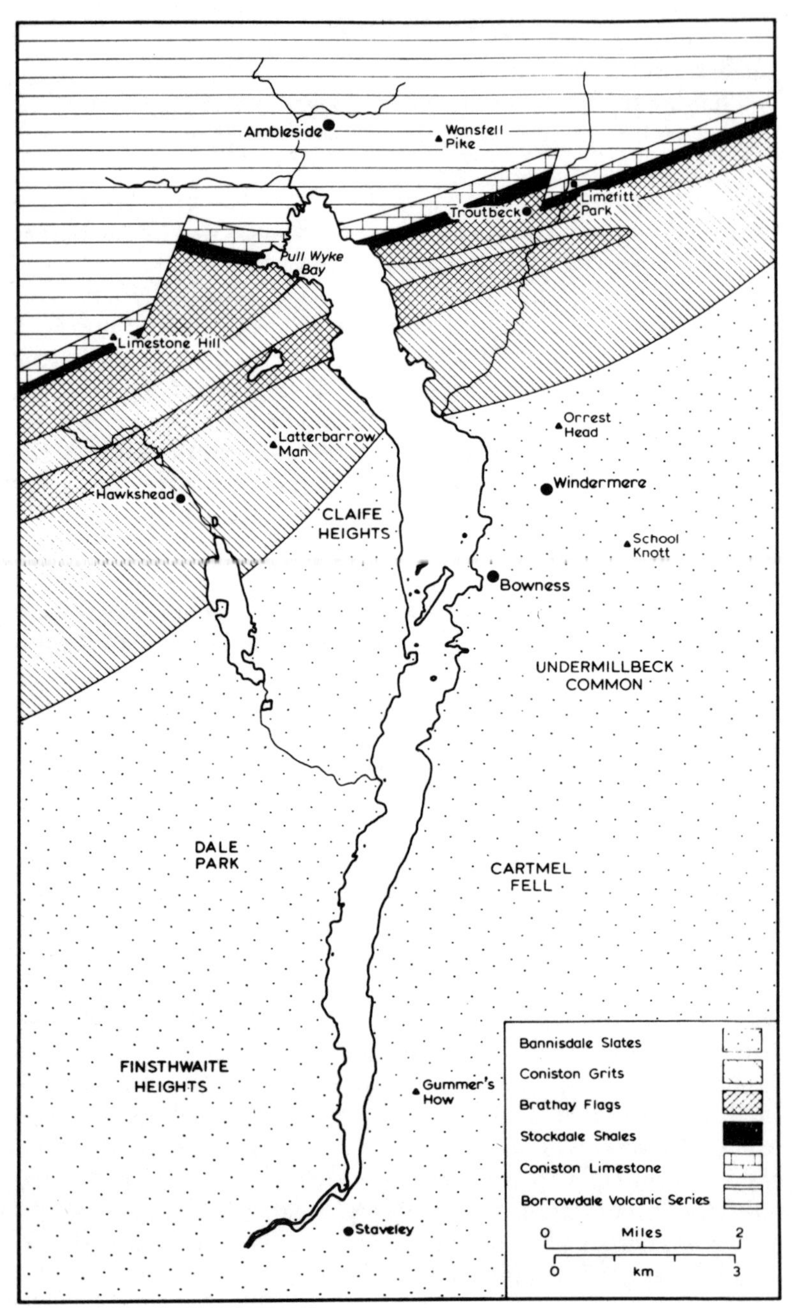

Geological map of the Windermere area

northern end of the lake has been carved out of a relatively weak band of rock within the more resistant Stockdale Shales.

Not surprisingly, the majority of buildings in the Windermere area are built with local freestone from the Silurian beds and consequently blend in well with their natural surroundings. Many small, abandoned quarries can be located throughout the area on the Silurian beds – quarries such as Rayrigg Quarry, just north of Bowness, on the local Bannisdale Slates. But it is the well-bedded and laminated Silurian mudstones which have been most successfully worked for building-stone in the area. The finely bedded mudstones comprising the Brathay Flags have, in the past, been worked both in extensive quarries which can be easily spotted on the eastern side of the Garburn Road above Troutbeck Church, and to the south of Skel Ghyll, above the Low Wood Hotel, where the fields are dotted with numerous small abandoned workings. Indeed, the largest slate quarries in the North of England – the Burlington Quarries at Kirkby, near Broughton in Furness – are found on the Brathay Flags. To many, this 'Westmorland Blue Slate' seems a dull stone for building purposes, yet while the dark bluey-grey flags, tinged with reddish-brown patches of iron staining, give the local buildings a rather subdued and solemn appearance, the local stone is not without a beauty and dignity of its own.

Today, building-stone can be easily transported ten or twenty miles from the large working quarries at Kirkby or Broughton Moor, but in former years the high cost of transport prohibited anything but the most local of outcrops being worked. In the neighbourhood of Hawkshead, for instance, roofing slates were nearly always obtained from the quarry on Borwick Ground Fell, while flags for floors and walls were worked at Coldwell and Brathay Quarries near Pull Wyke. These flags were also used for field boundaries, and rows of up-ended flags can still be seen lining the roadsides north and south of the village and in several other localities including Hawkshead churchyard and near Rothay Bridge, Ambleside. These same dull grey slates are seen again in the numerous dry-stone walls which stride up the hillsides flanking the Windermere valley, blending imperceptibly into the outcrops of rock which they frequently cross on the steeper slopes.

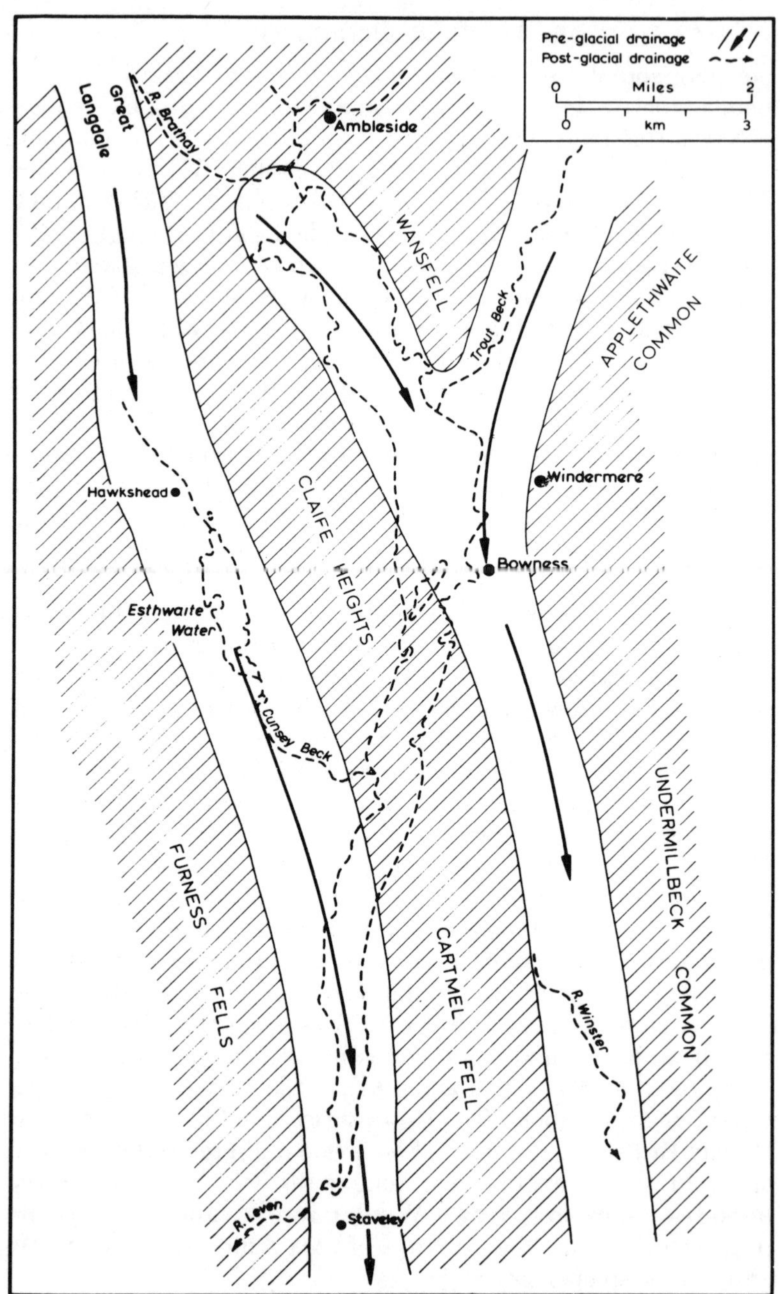

Pre-glacial drainage pattern in the Windermere area

Whilst the geology of the district has undoubtedly had a marked effect on the landforms and buildings of the Windermere area, there is very little evidence of any commercial exploitation of the local rocks other than for building-stone or for road chippings. Minerals are usually associated with areas of volcanic activity, and as a result very few workable mineral deposits have been discovered in the sedimentary rocks of the Silurian series. However, a number of small local volcanic intrusions have, in the past, resulted in a limited amount of prospecting. Records show that an old working located on the west side of Dale Park Beck, just above Thwaite Head, was mined for silver and lead around 1760, and there are the remains of a number of copper workings near Holmes Head Farm on Pull Beck, and on the side of Parks Gill above Hawkshead Hill. But in general Windermere has never been an important mining centre, and unlike neighbouring Coniston the area has never been blighted by the unsightly scars of waste tips and abandoned mine workings.

While the rocks themselves influenced the basic shape of the rolling hills of Southern Lakeland, it is the rivers and streams which have performed the major task of carving out the path of the deep valleys which today form such a prominent feature of the landscape. The evolution of the drainage pattern in the Windermere area is no less complex than its geological history, and the pattern formed by today's rivers is quite different from the radial pattern initiated during the Tertiary era, when the rivers and streams began to drain outwards in all directions from the highest part of the Lake District dome. These rivers rapidly cut down to form deep valleys, with steep gradients and little valley floor – quite different from the gentle gradients and wide floors of the main valleys today.

In the Windermere area the rivers draining southwards off the Lake District dome formed a series of steep-sided parallel valleys, flowing almost in straight lines from north to south. The main Windermere valley – which today has a forty-five-degree bend in its northern reach opposite Belle Grange – was almost certainly divided into two valleys at this stage of its development. A ridge of high land separating these two main valleys formed a continuous watershed running from Claife Heights to Cartmel Fell, crossing the line of the present valley where the lake has its shallow middle reach. To the west of this watershed, the course of the first valley followed a line running through Esthwaite Water and the southern reach of Windermere below Silver Holme. Beyond Lakeside, the Backbarrow Gorge had not yet come into being, and the valley continued its straight path southwards, reaching Morecambe Bay via Cartmel and Cark.

The valley occupied today by the northern reach of Windermere was, at this stage, merely a small right-hand tributary to a second major valley – which ran along a fault-guided course followed by the present line of the Trout Beck above Troutbeck Bridge, and continuing almost due south to join the present course of the River Winster. The Troutbeck Fault, whose 'shatter belt' of weakened rock was quickly exploited by the running water, was formed when the land to the west was moved northwards – offsetting the belt of Coniston Limestone by over half a mile where it crosses the fault-line north of Limefitt Park. Like the Backbarrow Gorge, the low col followed by the railway line east of Windermere Station did not exist at that time, and the high land stretching from Applethwaite Common to Undermillbeck Common formed a continuous watershed, dropping away on its eastern side to yet another north-south valley, followed by the present course of the River Kent above Staveley, and continuing due south through Crook and Underbarrow to the Lyth Valley.

This network of rivers and streams – with its series of steep-sided valleys running from north to south down the southern flank of the Lake District dome – was to form the dominant drainage pattern of the Windermere area for over 200 million years. Indeed, the present courses of the rivers and the becks of Southern Lakeland can best be understood if regarded as a relatively recent modification of this regional pattern, resulting from the effects of the Pleistocene glaciation on the Windermere area.

With the initial build-up of the Lake District ice-cap occurring some 500,000 years ago and the last glaciers retreating from the Windermere valley only 13,000 years ago, the Pleistocene or Quaternary glaciation is, in geological terms, a very recent event indeed. Consequently the marks left by the ice are still very fresh and can easily be identified by anyone who knows roughly what to look for. Yet, in order to appreciate the work of the ice in sculpting and moulding the landscape, we must realize that the Pleistocene glaciation – lasting nearly half a million years in the North of England – was not in fact one glaciation at all but a whole complex series of advances and retreats of the ice. In Britain the Pleistocene Ice Age consisted of at least three major glaciations separated by long interglacial periods which were often warmer than today's climate. Even this threefold division is a gross over-simplification as each of the major glaciations was itself composed of many minor advances of the ice, interspersed by warmer 'interstadials'.

The first major advance – the Anglian glaciation – occurred about 400,000 years ago. Vast depths of ice accumulated not only on the mountains of the Lake District but also on the Grampians and the North West Highlands, the Southern Uplands, the Pennines and the Welsh Mountains. From these high collecting grounds, the ice slowly advanced forwards onto the neighbouring basins of lowland Britain. At their maximum extent, the ice sheets stretched as far south as Gloucester and St Albans, and both the Irish Sea and the North Sea were completely filled with ice. The Anglian glaciation was followed by a warmer period known as the Hoxnian interglacial, whose milder climate – not unlike today's – lasted some 20 to 25 thousand years. During this warmer spell, the glaciers retreated and the ice melted, leaving the Lake District pocked by ice-scoured hollows and strewn with rocky glacial debris.

About 200,000 years ago the ice advanced again, marking the beginning of the Wolstonian glaciation which was to last for about 70,000 years. Once again, as the mean annual temperature fell by some 7 or 8°C, the amount of precipitation actually decreased, but a much greater proportion of it fell as snow, especially in the winter months. The snow accumulated on the high ground of Central Lakeland as firn or névé and, as the summer temperatures were inadequate to melt all of the preceding winter's fall, the névé gradually accumulated from one year to the next. Over a period of many years, the pressure caused by the increasing weight of snow gradually compacted its lower layers into ice and in time began to force the accumulating

Major Glacial and Interglacial periods during the Pleistocene

mass of ice downhill due to gravity. In this manner the ice moved out of the upland hollows where it had collected and started its ponderous journey down the existing valleys, gradually filling these river courses to a depth of hundreds of feet and converting them into vast streams of slowly moving ice.

This time, the ice sheets reached as far south as the Midlands before another warmer spell checked their growth. The following interglacial period – the Ipswichian – lasted some fifteen thousand years, during which the ice completely disappeared and the temperatures were much higher than at present. The southern Lake District probably enjoyed a short period of sub-tropical warmth, as remains discovered only forty miles away at

Victoria Cave near Settle, in 1845, showed conclusively that hippopotamuses, rhinoceroses, lions and elephants lived in the North of England at this time. Due to the melting of the ice sheets over the whole of the northern hemisphere, there was more water in the world's oceans at this period than at any other time before or since. As a result of this rise in sea level, the lower portions of the Kent, the Winster and the Leven valleys were each flooded during this, and subsequent, interglacials. The Lyth Valley, and the Winster Valley below Bowland Bridge, became narrow inlets of Morecambe Bay itself, whilst the estuary of the River Leven extended right up to the present gorge above Haverthwaite.

Once again, around 115,000 years ago, the climate reverted to Polar conditions and remained extremely cold for some 100,000 years. The maximum advance of the ice sheets occurred towards the end of this period, when, following a rapid build-up of ice, the Late Devensian glaciation reached its peak approximately 18,000 years ago. Although it was not the most extensive of the major ice advances, this episode probably left a greater imprint on the Windermere landscape than any other glaciation preceding it. Not only did the Late Devensian advance destroy the remains of the previous glaciations, but it also left its own extensive debris – most of which has remained in place until the present day.

Since the ice finally melted in the Windermere valley some thirteen thousand years ago, there have been several colder spells. Ice accumulated yet again in the uplands of the Central Fells during the 'Loch Lomond Advance' of the Younger Dryas period, roughly ten thousand years ago, but although the ice reached the head of Langdale and deposited a jumbled mass of morainic material on the floor of Mickleden, a further amelioration of the climate ensured that the glaciers did not reach the Windermere area.

During each of these major glacial advances, the greatest accumulation of ice occurred on the highest areas of the Central Lakeland Fells – especially when snow collected in north- or east-facing hollows, where the almost continuous shadow prevented the sun from melting the newly fallen snow, even during the warmer summers. The ice which filled the

Windermere valley during the Pleistocene collected high up above the valleys of Langdale and Grasmere – in shallow depressions on the slopes of Bow Fell and Pike o'Blisco and beneath the summits of Fairfield and Hart Crag. As the ice was forced downhill by the great weight of snow accumulating on top, frost-shattered boulders held in the base of the ice scoured the hollows deeper and wider. The resulting corrie basins often became filled with water after the ice melted, and even today Stickle Tarn, Easedale Tarn and Blea Tarn continue to occupy hollows which were once the gathering grounds of major glaciers.

At the onset of the Anglian glaciation the existing river valleys ran roughly north-south, and as the ice spilled over from the corrie basins, it moved southwards along these deep, narrow valleys. It is more than likely that, at this stage of the Pleistocene, the Windermere valley was occupied by two separate glaciers. At the height of the glaciation, very little of the Cumbrian Mountains would have projected above the ice-cap, and a huge river of ice – over two thousand feet deep – would have moved slowly down Great Langdale, away from the gathering grounds below Rossett Pike and Crinkle Crags. This enormous glacier would have been joined at Skelwith Bridge by ice moving down Little Langdale, and at some periods by ice coming down the Grasmere valley and spilling across the low col at Red Bank. The floors of these valleys would each have been several hundred feet higher than at present, and as the glaciers completely choked one valley, the ice would have been ponded back and would have spilled over the lowest part of the neighbouring watershed to follow a new course. As a result, the paths of the glaciers changed many times during the Ice Age, and it seems likely that, at this early stage, the ice from Langdale and Grasmere moved southwards from Skelwith Bridge following the existing river valley and carved out the steep-sided valley whose extensive floor is now occupied in part by Esthwaite Water and the lower reaches of Windermere below Rawlinson Nab.

The ice which occupied the upper reaches of Windermere north of Belle Grange had its origin in the high collecting grounds of Rydal Fell and Scandale Fell. As the ice moved southwards beyond Ambleside and towards Troutbeck Bridge, it joined what was at that time probably a larger glacier flowing along the floor of the main Troutbeck valley. This glacier was formed of ice which had collected on the slopes of Caudale Moor and Park Fell and had moved south, straddling the resistant summit of Troutbeck Tongue and eroding a deep trough to the north of Troutbeck Church. The combined ice flow continued to follow a path southwards down the existing river valley to the east of Bowness, deepening and widening the floor of the Winster valley before breaking up to join the ice floes of Morecambe Bay. Further to the east another major glacier inched its way along Kentmere and down the Lyth valley, while to the west a smaller river of ice crept down Grizedale to enter the frozen sea south of Haverthwaite.

The evidence which suggests that two glaciers flowed down the Windermere valley at this stage, is found in the present form of the Windermere trough. A quick glance at the Ordnance Survey map of the area reveals that Windermere itself consists not of one but of two deeply eroded basins, separated by a relatively shallow stretch of lake bed, dotted with islands in the vicinity of Bowness Bay. The presence of these two discrete basins, severed by an extensive area of water less than ten feet deep in many places, strongly suggests that, at this early period at least, the Windermere valley was being carved out by two distinct glaciers. Only at a later stage, as the ice was ponded back and created a new course, were the two basins joined together to form the foundations of the longest lake bed in England.

During the tens of thousands of years that these huge glaciers moved across the area, the ice was relentlessly grinding and smashing its path through the existing narrow river valleys, creating wider and deeper troughs in order to accommodate the immense volume of ice. The erosion usually attributed to these glaciers was not, however, directly due to the abrasive action of the ice itself but rather due to the effect of jagged stones and boulders which had fallen onto the glacier surface from neighbouring slopes and which were then carried underneath the ice or along the outer margins of the glacier. These protruding rocks acted like a giant nailfile, scraping and scratching the bedrock whenever they came into contact with the valley sides or the valley floor. The scratches or 'striations' which resulted can often still be seen today where rocky knolls rear up from the valley floors or where patches of bare rock outcrop on the valley sides. The small grooves etched onto the rocky outcrop just south of the landing stage on Ferry Nab, for instance, can be quite clearly made out to be striations, as the scratches do not follow the direction of the natural lines of geological weakness picked out by weathering but are clearly aligned from north to south – the direction in which the ice flowed at this point.

In addition to this grinding action by the rock particles which were solidly embedded in the base of the ice, a great deal of powerful erosion was accomplished by turbulent torrents of meltwater actually flowing beneath the ice itself. As a result of this tremendous erosional activity, the Windermere, Esthwaite and Troutbeck valleys all exhibit the typical steep sides and wide, gently undulating valley floors characteristic of glacially eroded troughs. Each of these valleys was also hollowed out in places to produce deep basins which were subsequently filled with water after the ice melted. Both the main basins of the Windermere valley were eroded to a depth well below the present sea level – the northern basin reaching a maximum depth of 80 feet below present sea level (209 feet below present lake level), and the southern basin attaining a depth of 8 feet below sea level (137 feet below lake level). The ice filling the Esthwaite valley gouged out a deep basin which is now occupied by Esthwaite Water and its adjacent tarns, while the Troutbeck valley also contained a deep trough occupied, after the ice melted, by a lake stretching roughly $1\frac{1}{2}$ miles upstream from Limefitt to Troutbeck Park.

During the Wolstonian and Late Devensian glaciations, a number of modifications to the ice flow resulted in changes to the drainage pattern which have left their mark to the present day. As the glaciers moved southwards down their steep-sided troughs, they must, on many occasions, have been prevented from entering Morecambe Bay by the vast accumulation of pack ice moving south and east across the Irish Sea. As the Windermere ice became ponded back, it must eventually have spilled across the lowest parts of the watershed, flowing over into neighbouring valleys in its attempt to reach the sea. Many low cols must have been breached in this way, including the series of cols between the Winster and Gilpin valleys – one occupied today by Knipe Tarn. The low col followed by the Garburn Pass between Troutbeck and Kentmere was no doubt deepened by a similar process when the Troutbeck glacier was ponded back and spilled over into the Kentmere valley.

Most of these glacial spillways acted merely as temporary safety valves, but occasionally the ice was ponded back to such an extent that the spillway became a permanent feature of the drainage pattern. At some stage during the Pleistocene glaciation, the ice moving southwards down the Windermere and Troutbeck valleys spilled eastwards over the existing watershed near the present site of Windermere Station. The ice continued to follow this path for thousands of years, lowering the col by hundreds of feet and, in the process, eroding a deep, wide valley. Although this course was eventually abandoned by the ice in favour of a more southerly route, the resulting valley has remained – its undulating floor occupied today not only by the River Gowan but also by the main road and railway line from Kendal.

An event which was to have even more important repercussions on the local landscape occurred at the northern end of the Windermere valley when the main body of ice from the Langdale and Grasmere valleys became ponded back and began to flow eastwards beyond Skelwith Bridge into the neighbouring Windermere valley, instead of following its previous course southwards along the Esthwaite valley. It may well have been at this time that the newly combined regimes of ice from the Langdale, Grasmere, Rydal, Scandale and Troutbeck valleys proved too powerful for the Winster and Gowan valleys to contain. Whatever the cause, the ice in the main Windermere valley abandoned its previous route and pushed its way southwards across the main Claife Heights – Cartmel Fell watershed, finally breaching the high land which had separated the two Windermere basins and carving out the deep trough which today joins the northern and southern reaches of Windermere in the vicinity of Bowness Bay.

On both sides of the Windermere valley, numerous waterfalls occur where tributary streams – hanging high above the glacially overdeepened trough – have attempted to erode their valleys down to the main floor. The impressive falls at Stock Ghyll Force and the picturesque cascades of Wynlass Beck were formed in this way, and while the smaller streams draining Claife Heights and Cartmel Fell simply plunge from boulder to boulder in a mad helter-skelter course down the sheer valley sides, the more powerful Trout Beck has cut back a deeply incised gorge above Troutbeck Bridge in an attempt to lower the floor of its valley to the level of Windermere itself.

Another glacial spillway was formed when the outlet into Morecambe Bay became blocked by ice moving down the Kent estuary. The meltwater draining from the Windermere glacier rapidly became ponded back to form an ice-dammed lake, which ultimately spilled over the watershed, cutting a winding channel across the high land between Newby Bridge and Haverthwaite, before reaching the sea near Greenodd. With the gradual melting of the ice in the Kent estuary, this channel was abandoned during the subsequent interglacial period, but striations high up on the sides of the valley show that the resulting Backbarrow Gorge (together with neighbouring valleys at Finsthwaite and Canny Hill) served as a spillway for ice leaving the Windermere valley during a later glacial advance. As the Windermere glacier finally melted and retreated some thirteen thousand years ago, the former valley floor south of Staveley was blocked by mounds of glacial moraine, and the river draining Windermere adopted the newer course across the former watershed at Backbarrow. Subsequently the River Leven has deepened this gorge further, cutting down approximately forty feet since the end of the Pleistocene and breaching the extensive ridges of terminal moraine which run across the valley floor just north of Newby Bridge.

While glacial erosion was the main agent which modified the local drainage pattern during the Pleistocene, glacial deposition also left its stamp clearly on the Windermere landscape. As the vast rivers of ice moved down the valleys, they carried with them huge amounts of glacial till – ranging in size from large, angular, frost-shattered boulders to finely ground morainic clay – which was left stranded wherever the ice melted. In the Troutbeck valley an extensive area of low morainic mounds was deposited on the valley floor north of Troutbeck Park, whilst the valley side above Troutbeck village is masked by hummocky morainic material. To the east of Brant Fell a low ridge of terminal moraine straddles the valley just north of the road to Crook, marking a stage in the retreat of the ice from the Winster valley, while the floor of the Esthwaite valley near Outgate is blanketed by low mounds of glacial boulder clay.

Many of the valley floors in the Windermere area are covered by glacial till which was moulded *underneath* the moving ice to leave long, oval-shaped mounds – fifty to a hundred feet high – when the ice finally melted. There are numerous examples of these 'drumlins' in the Esthwaite valley, both to the south of Hawkshead village and beside Cunsey Beck, and Esthwaite Water itself almost completely surrounds two of these rounded hillocks. A number of these conspicuous mounds are found in the Gowan valley between Staveley and Ings, while probably the most celebrated drumlin of all is Queen Adelaide's Hill, which rises 130 feet above the lake shore, providing an excellent vantage point overlooking the upper and middle reaches of the lake.

Since the most recent retreat of the ice, only thirteen thousand years ago, there has been very little time for nature to modify the landscape further. Yet extensive post-glacial deposition of river sediments has reduced the size of all the glacially eroded lakes and has caused some of them to disappear completely. In immediate post-glacial times, Esthwaite Water was both longer and wider than it is today and stretched nearly a mile further north towards Hawkshead Hall. Where the lake has been infilled, the valley floor has since been drained and is utilized today by a large car-park, the Hawkshead relief road and a local camp site. Near Matson Ground, to the east of Bowness, an extensive flat area of alluvial deposits marks the floor of a former ice-scoured lake bed, whilst in the Troutbeck valley the former lake stretching from Limefitt to Troutbeck Park has been completely filled in by post-glacial river gravels.

Windermere itself was considerably longer in immediate post-glacial times, extending upstream almost as far as Rydal village. Post-glacial deposits of alluvium created the extensive flat valley floor on which Rothay Park now stands, and even today the delta of the River Brathay continues to extend outwards

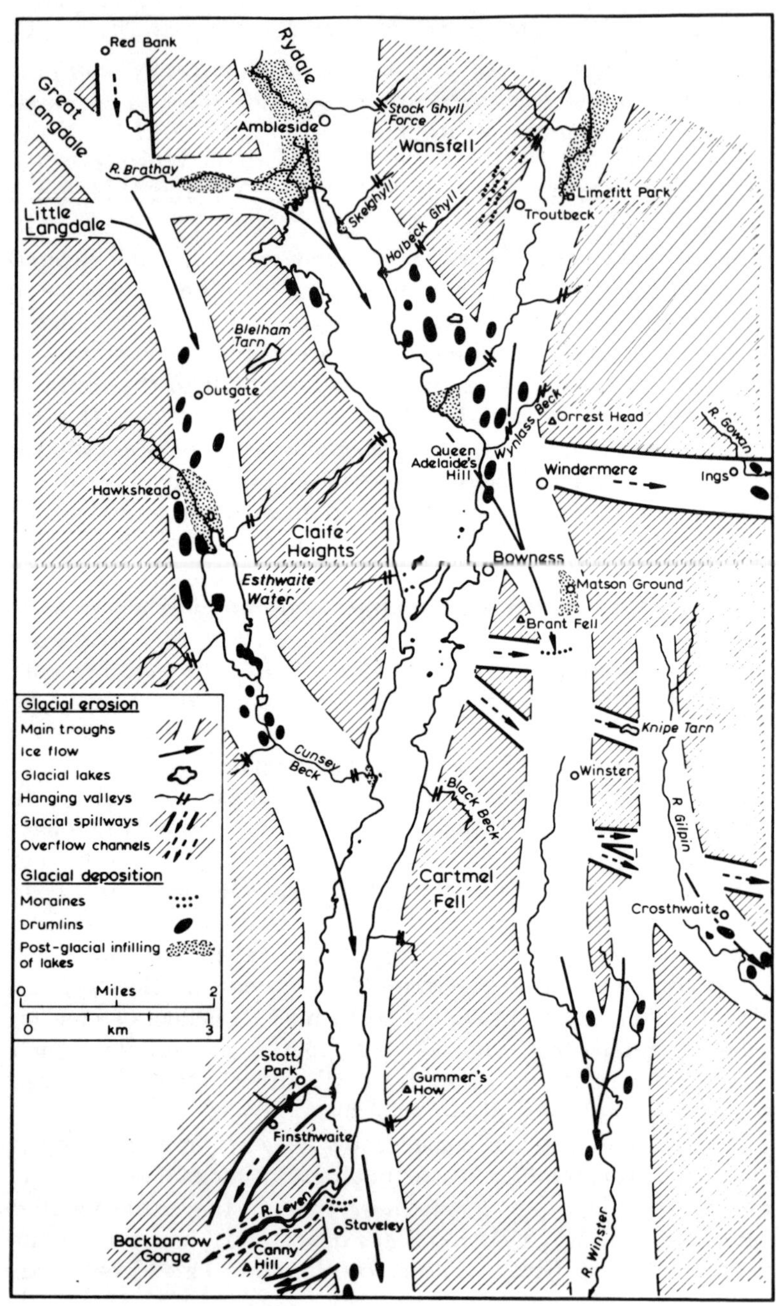

Glacial landforms in the Windermere area

across the lake. This process of post-glacial deposition can be gauged more accurately by taking cores of mud from the lake bed – a project undertaken under the auspices of the Freshwater Biological Association by Dr Winifred Pennington in the 1950s. These cores revealed that the top twelve to fifteen feet of fine brownish mud have accumulated since the ice completely disappeared thirteen thousand years ago. Beneath this mud, alternate layers of silt, sand and clay – known as 'varves' – represent the seasonal accumulation of river deposits during the colder late-glacial climate. The coarser material in these layers was deposited by summer meltwaters, whilst the lower flow of the winter months was sufficient to carry only clay-sized particles onto the lake bed. These annual deposits can be dated – in much the same way as counting tree-rings – and by this analysis the lake sediments can yield details of the local climate and vegetation from the melting of the ice right up to the present day.

Using this method we can identify and date the beginning of the clearance of the Lake District forests by the first settlers – marked by an increase in the organic material contained in the lake-bed sediments. And through the lasting record of the Windermere mud, the vicissitudes of the post-glacial climate can be revealed for detailed scrutiny.

4

Early Settlers

Towards the end of the Late Devensian period, the climate of the Windermere area slowly started to improve. As the winter snowfall decreased and the summer temperatures gradually climbed higher, the glaciers began to melt and to retreat up-valley. By c.11,000 BC the gradual amelioration of the climate had resulted in the complete disappearance of the Lake District ice-cap, and dwarf willows, juniper and birches began to colonize the valley floors as the area experienced the milder weather conditions of post-glacial times. It would be a mistake, however, to imagine that the mild, moist conditions have remained unchanged right up to the present day. Indeed the opposite is true, as the climate has been in a continual state of fluctuation ever since the ice vanished.

Although generally the climate has been relatively mild since the glaciers disappeared from the Windermere and Troutbeck valleys, there have been a number of much colder periods – some long, some short – in the last thirteen thousand years. Perhaps the severest of these cold spells occurred between 8,800 and 8,300 BC, when the record preserved in the lake-bed sediments reveals that the ice-cap returned to the highest peaks of Lakeland. During this mini-glaciation the ice did not reach as far as the Windermere valley, but small glaciers spilled down into Great Langdale from the corrie hollows on the slopes beside Rossett Gill and Stake Pass to deposit low, hummocky mounds of glacial till at the head of Mickleden. Other, less severe cold spells occurred when the climate deteriorated at the end of the fourth century and during the thirteenth century. During Elizabethan times contemporary paintings often reflect the colder conditions of the age, while even Shakespeare's poetry reminds us of the seventeenth-century 'Little Ice Age' when milk frequently came 'frozen home in pail'. As recently as 1963 the whole of Windermere was frozen over for several weeks, and skaters were able to glide across to Belle Isle.

The freezing conditions frequently experienced in winter today should serve to remind us that the present climate is not all that different from the climate which prevailed during the Pleistocene glaciation. The low-lying Windermere valley is generally kept quite warm by the mild, moist air blown in across the North Atlantic, and snow rarely stays on the valley floor for more than a few days. But the situation is very different two or three thousand feet above the floor of Langdale or Rydale. Already snow beds lie for nine or ten months of the year in some north-facing hollows, and it would only require a drop of 3 or 4°C throughout the year to create a permanent ice-cap on Scafell, Bowfell or Helvellyn. Because the Furness Fells shelter the area from the rain-bearing south-westerly winds, Windermere receives only about forty inches of precipitation annually, and little of this usually falls as snow. But in the exposed higher fells, precipitation is much greater, and a higher proportion falls as snow. Although Seathwaite, in the Borrowdale valley, holds the dubious reputation of being the wettest settlement in England (with 140 inches per annum), far higher precipitation undoubtedly falls on the higher slopes. With such an extensive volume of snow falling on the higher Central Fells above Windermere, it would take only a relatively small deterioration in today's climate to revert to the conditions of the Late Devensian glaciation. In fact, the climatic records show that during the twentieth century we have been enjoying one of the warmest of the milder spells which have occurred since the ice retreated some thirteen thousand years ago. During the opening years of this century the climate became progressively warmer, and during the 1940s Britain experienced the hottest summers for two hundred years. Since 1950 the tide has turned, and the climate has been getting progressively cooler and wetter. Over the last twenty or thirty years many European glaciers have been re-advancing down their valleys, and the gradual deterioration of the British climate has led many experts to believe that the return of the Lake District ice-cap is imminent.

As well as colder spells scattered across the last ten thousand years of the climatic records, the Lake District has also enjoyed lengthy periods during post-glacial times when temperatures have been considerably warmer than at present. Following the final disappearance of the ice, the climate gradually warmed up from c. 8,000 BC until a climatic 'optimum' was reached in c. 3,000 BC. At the height of this sub-Boreal period, the average summer temperatures were approximately 2°C higher than today's, and the winters were milder by at least 1°C. Due to the greater warmth, trees flourished high up on the valley sides, and woodlands of sessile oak and elm reached a thousand feet above the present tree line, while ash dominated on the damper valley floors. Not only was it warmer in the third millennium BC but the climate was also drier than at present, making the uplands less waterlogged and more suitable for grazing.

It was during this climatic optimum that the first human settlers arrived in the Lake District.

Archaeological evidence suggests that man first settled in the South of England before the ice finally retreated from the Lake District and the Scottish Uplands. Due to the enormous volume of water locked up in the ice sheets of the northern hemisphere at this time, the sea level around Britain was some seventy to a hundred feet lower than at present, and the English Channel – if it existed at all – formed only a narrow and shallow barrier to potential settlers from the Continent. Across this land bridge palaeolithic man migrated to his new territory, and remains dating from this period have been discovered as far north as Derbyshire. But it was not until some eight thousand years after the glaciers had finally retreated from the Windermere valley that early settlers began to appear on the fringes of the Lake District. These neolithic people arrived c.3.000 BC, making their first settlements on the undulating lowlands of Low Furness and along the Cumberland coastal plain.

Within a short time neolithic settlements had spread into the very heart of the Lake District, and remains from this New Stone Age culture have been widely recovered from the Windermere area. While the neolithic settlers were undoubtedly skilled hunters, they were also the first people to develop sedentary forms of agriculture. Consequently large areas of oak, elm and pine were cleared from the valley floors and the lower valley sides to create fields for crops. The clearance of these woodlands is once again faithfully recorded by the increase of organic material in the sediments recovered from the bed of Windermere. As well as growing their own food, the neolithic people kept cattle and used stone axes to build dug-out canoes for fishing. To supplement their diets they hunted deer, wolves, foxes and rabbits with stone-tipped arrows and then used stone knives to skin the animals before making the skins into clothing.

Although there are no remains of large neolithic 'henge' monuments – such as the Castlerigg stone circle – in the Windermere area, nevertheless many stone axes, arrowheads and knives – collectively called 'celts' – have been unearthed in the local area at High Wray, near Windermere Station and at Chapel Ridding. The discovery of a neolithic stone axe factory high up on the slopes of Great Langdale, in 1947, revealed the source of stone axe heads which have been located as far afield as the Yorkshire Dales, the Isle of Man and the south coast of England. This well-organized industry exploited a particularly hard band of volcanic rock below the summit of Pike o'Stickle, and the finished celts were transported from here down Langdale before, in all probability, being shipped along the length of Windermere to reach the coast. The discovery of a Langdale axe head near Troutbeck village has also led some experts to suggest that the 'Roman' road over High Street may already have been in existence for the neolithic axe traffic long before the Romans arrived.

By c.2,000 BC the traditional stone implements began to be supplemented with bronze articles. This metal-working technology spread gradually across Britain from northern Germany and heralded the new culture of the Bronze Age. Although there are many Bronze Age burial mounds on the Lakeland foothills, there is a distinct lack of these tumuli on the fells surrounding Windermere – an absence explained, perhaps, by the destruction of evidence through centuries of farming. In all probability there *were* Bronze Age farmers in the locality, but remains of this culture are limited to two sites – one west of Hawkshead and another in the Troutbeck valley. The Bronze Age cairn high up on the moor above Hawkshead Hill was found to contain cremated remains and a flint knife when it was excavated in 1883. This discovery of a *stone* knife in a *Bronze* Age burial mound demonstrates how the later culture only gradually replaced the former, as the ideas and technology of the Continental beaker people were slowly assimilated by the native inhabitants of northern England. In contrast, the Bronze Age tumulus at Woundale in the Upper Troutbeck valley contained a number of bronze implements, and many bronze weapons have been discovered over the years both at Troutbeck and at Ambleside.

Towards the end of the Bronze Age period, c.700 BC, the climate once again became colder and wetter. Settlements on the higher fells were abandoned, and their inhabitants moved down into the valleys. It was shortly after this climatic deterioration that Iron Age technology began to be adopted in Britain. Like the Bronze Age culture before it, the Iron Age took hundreds of years to spread throughout the country. While iron-making technology dominated the Midlands and South East of England by the time of Christ, the Iron Age culture was by no means universally adopted when the Romans arrived. Pockets of Bronze Age culture survived into the Iron Age, especially in the North West where the Brigantes – a native Celtic tribe – inhabited the area.

It was a local band of these Celtic warriors who were responsible for the construction of the rectangular earthwork which today crowns the top of Allen Knott, a prominent summit a mile north of Orrest Head. This resistant ridge lying on an outcrop of Brathay Flags constitutes a first-rate defensive site, with extensive views across the Troutbeck valley and along Windermere. Much of the southern flank of this hill fort has been obliterated by cultivation, and part of the eastern side was destroyed by quarrying earlier this century. Nevertheless, the north-west corner of the rampart can still be easily traced, forming an embankment some eight feet wide and up to seven feet high. A section cut through the rampart in 1963 revealed a dry-stone facing enclosing a core of loose boulders set in an earth filling. Whether the hill fort was constructed before or after the Roman occupation is uncertain, but it is quite possible that the earthwork was thrown up in the troubled times preceding the

Roman invasion in order to protect the local Brigantes from the attacks of other marauding tribes such as the Novantae from across the Solway.

The invasion of Britain by the Emperor Claudius in AD 43 marked the first real challenge to Brigantian supremacy in the North of England. The Roman legions quickly overran the South East of England, and by AD 47 they were able to establish a temporary frontier along the line of the Fosse Way from Cirencester to Lincoln. But it took nearly forty years to conquer the Celtic tribes of Highland Britain. In AD 78 Agricola overcame the resistance of the Silures in Central Wales and the Ordovices of North Wales, and in the following year the Romans turned their attention to the North of England. The Lake District was systematically occupied as Agricola's troops marched north, and the Romans established their most northerly boundary between the Clyde and the Forth in AD 80. In AD 126 Emperor Hadrian constructed the wall from Bowness-on-Solway to Wallsend-on-Tyne, and this later frontier remained the boundary of Romanization almost continuously until it was abandoned in about AD 383, shortly before the Romans left Britain.

During this 250-year period the Lake District formed part of the Roman 'Military Zone', whose seventy forts and three legionary fortresses were designed to protect the 'Civil Zone' of south-east England from the barbarian tribes to the north. The Northern Military Zone was devoid of any real towns. Even Corstopitum (Corbridge) and Luguvalium (Carlisle) were little more than military garrisons, although each contained a small civil settlement. The success of the Hadrianic frontier policy depended on fast, efficient communications between each of the smaller forts and the great northern legionary centres at Deva (Chester) and Eburacum (York). The local forts housed a garrison of one cohort – a division of about five or six hundred men – and each fort was able to call-up reinforcements quickly from the nearest legionary headquarters. The main route up the west coast ran from Chester, via Ribchester and Kendal, to Carlisle. At Alavna (the Roman fort at Watercrook just south of Kendal) another route branched off to the west running via Galava (Ambleside) and Mediobogdum (Hardknott) to the coastal fort at Glannaventa (Ravenglass). The route of this

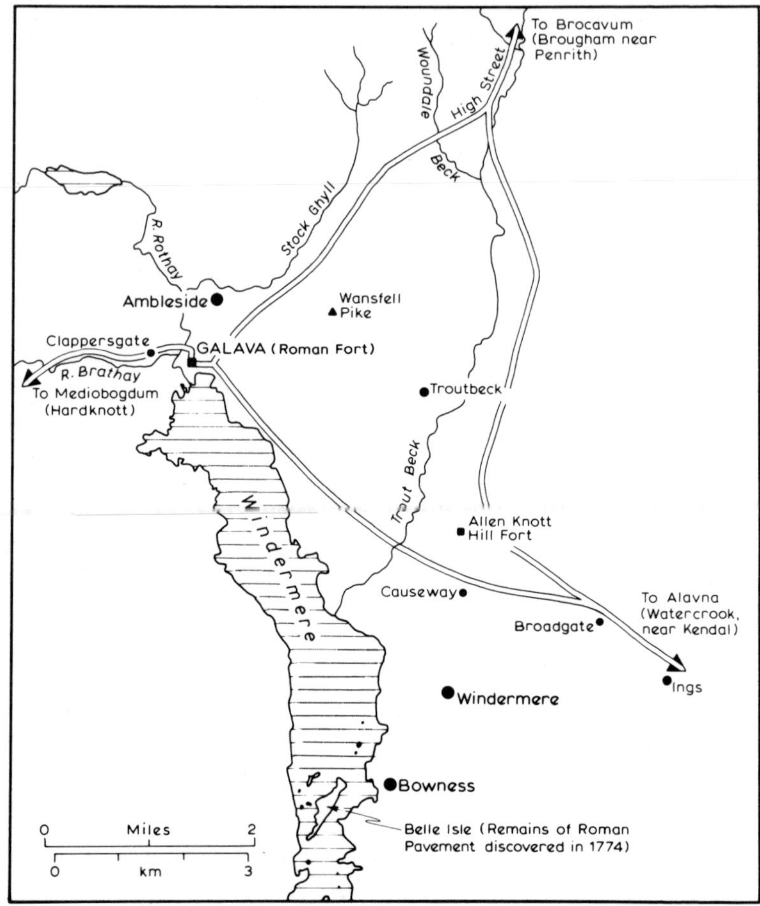

Probable line of Roman roads in the Windermere area

Roman road has never been traced with any great certainty, but it probably followed the Kent and Gowan valleys before cutting across the northern flank of Banner Rigg and Orrest Head *en route* to Waterhead. Although there are no stone foundations to prove it, local names such as Broadgate ('Broad street') and Causeway suggest that the memory of a local Roman road may well have been in the minds of the first settlers who farmed this area a thousand years ago.

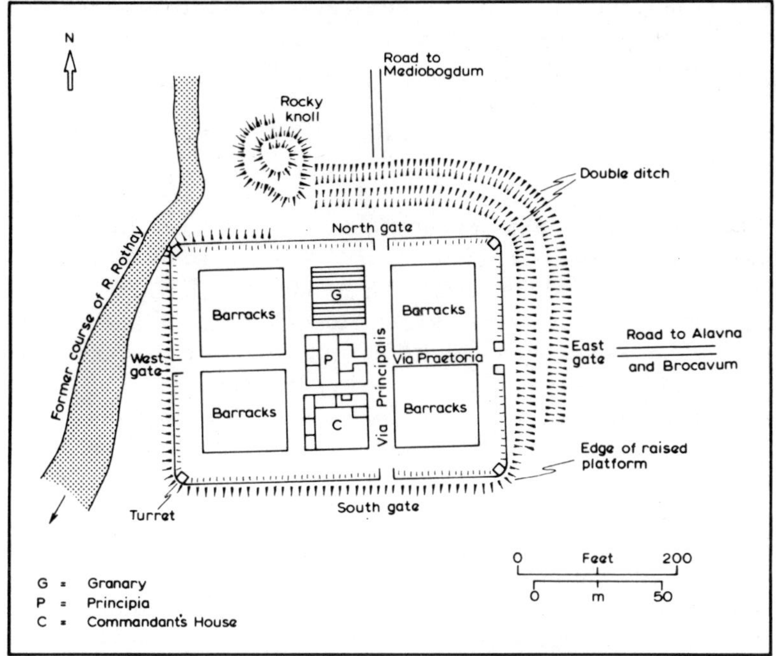

The Roman fort at Galava, near Waterhead, Ambleside

Where the main Alavna-Galava road crossed the Troutbeck valley, another road branched north, being joined at The Tongue by a direct route from the Ambleside fort across the northern slopes of Wansfell. From this point the highway gradually climbed the eastern slopes of the Troutbeck valley to reach the summit of High Street. Today this section of the road can still be traced by following the line of a groove which makes its way steadily upwards to the plateau on the summit. Beyond High Street the road ran north to the Roman fort at Brocavum (Brougham, near Penrith), where it joined the main highway to the Wall. Whether the road over High Street was pioneered by the Romans or merely taken over by them for their own use is uncertain, but we are sure that the Romans were not the only travellers to have used this route. During the Middle Ages the Street was called 'Brettestrette' – 'the road of the Britons' – and

since the eighteenth century the local inhabitants have referred
to it as 'Scots' Rake' – a name harking back to the Scottish raids
of the twelfth century.

The most extensive Roman remains in the Windermere area
are found at Galava, the small Roman fort situated at the head
of Windermere where the route from Kendal to Ravenglass
turned west to cross the River Rothay. This small garrison,
situated on the alluvial floodplain at Borran's Field near
Waterhead, housed a cohort of five hundred soldiers and was
built by the Emperor Trajan in about AD 100 to replace an
earlier, smaller fort constructed by Agricola in AD 79. The fort was
erected on a rectangular platform built up above the flood level
using gravel dredged from the bed of Windermere. This raised
platform, forming a rectangle some 100 yards by 150 yards, was
surrounded by a wall with turrets at each of the four corners. The
road from Alavna entered the fort through the East Gate, while
to the north another gate led out towards Clappersgate and
Hardknott. On the landward side, to both the north and east, a
double ditch was constructed to protect the fort from attack. The
South Gate, whose sill is still virtually intact, looked out onto the
marsh, while to the west the Watergate led directly to the River
Rothay, which at that time flowed immediately beside the fort a
hundred yards to the east of its present course.

Inside the main East Gate, the Via Praetoria – flanked to
north and south by rows of barracks – led directly to the
Principia, the administrative centre of the fort. To the north
remains of the granaries can still be seen, while to the south the
commander's house consisted of some twelve rooms built around
a courtyard. The fort was solidly built, the freestone used to
construct its walls being brought from as far afield as Lancaster.
Excavations on the site have, however, revealed that the history
of the garrison was not entirely peaceful during Roman times.
The remains of not one but three floors, each lying on top of an
earlier foundation, indicate that the structure was burnt down
and rebuilt on more than one occasion, probably during the local
uprisings which occurred around AD 181 and 275.

To the north and north-east of the fort a small civilian
settlement grew up to service the garrison and to cater for its
everyday needs. The civil quarter probably included a

blacksmith, a leatherworker and a potter, and extensive remains of Roman pottery, leather shoes and bronze and similar items have been discovered here. Excavations made on the east side of Borrans Road in 1963 also unearthed a number of roughly cobbled stone pavements, probably forming the foundations of small houses or workshops. A Roman tombstone found in the garden of Wanlass How and many other remains from Galava are exhibited at the Lake District National Park Centre at Brockhole.

The only other site in the Windermere area where remains dating possibly from Roman times have been found is Belle Isle. In 1774 Thomas English, when constructing the foundations of his round house, recorded the discovery of a 'beautiful pavement, curiously paved with pebbles of small size'. If this was indeed a Roman pavement, the presence of a Roman building on Belle Isle would add weight to the likelihood that the Romans also used Windermere as an artery of communication – perhaps shipping in stone from the coast or carrying supplies of timber from High Furness.

When the Romans finally withdrew from Britain towards the end of the fourth century, this caused little immediate change in the lives of the majority of the local inhabitants of the Windermere area. Throughout their stay the Romans had maintained little more than a military presence in the area, and their effect on the local landscape had been minimal. After the Romans left, the native Celtic peoples carried on farming the hillsides and valleys in much the same way as they had done before the Romans arrived, rearing their sheep and planting their crops as their ancestors had done for centuries. The 'civilized' life of the Roman Empire had barely rubbed off on them, and even contemporary Roman accounts described the local herding and weaving which were to form the traditional Lakeland way of life for many centuries to come.

One effect of the Romans' departure did, however, have much wider implications: the withdrawal of the *pax Romana* created a military vacuum, resulting in a troubled period of internecine strife in northern England. As the Roman garrisons departed, the area was left open to the raids of the Scots from Ireland, and the Picts from Scotland. In order to defend themselves from attack, the native peoples of northern England banded together in an alliance whose powerful leaders – the descendants of the Celtic king Coel Hen – ruled the whole of the Pennines, as far north as Hadrian's Wall, during the fifth century. Towards the end of this century, the lands to the west of the Pennines – including the Windermere area – split away and became a separate kingdom, the kingdom of Rheged, stretching from the Clyde in the north to the Ribble in the south.

These Britannic Celts, descended from the same stock as the Celtic peoples of Wales and Cornwall, had strong historical and cultural links with their fellow Britons. The name 'Cumbria' itself signified the 'land of the Welsh', and much of the evidence for these Dark Ages of history has been passed down to us through Welsh poetry and folklore. The historical poems of the Welsh bard Taliesin tell us of one of these princes – Urien, King of Rheged – who defeated the Picts in the battle for Gwên Ystrad (the Vale of Eden) and became the most powerful king in Britain. After the Battle of Arderydd (Arthuret, ten miles north of Carlisle) in 573, Urien expanded his kingdom to include most of Cumberland and Westmorland, and by 580, at the height of his power, his armies were dominant from the Cheviots in the north to the borders of Gwent in the south.

The court of the kings of Rheged was a splendid affair, modelled on the manners of the Irish kingdoms and maintained by a continuance of the Roman tax system. The Court was filled with musicians and poets who celebrated the noble deeds of their kings and sang their praises in battle. This retinue was financed by levying a tribute of cattle, corn and other dues, which were collected by *cais* or revenue officers. Payments made by the local farmers of the Windermere area would have included *cowgeld*, a payment of cattle, and *cornage*, a tax composed of various foodstuffs. In order to maintain their armies, the princes of Rheged – in common with the other British kings – imposed a system of *dofraeth*, the billeting and maintenance of troops by the local population.

Ultimately the very success of the kingdom of Rheged led to intense personal jealousy, and Urien was treacherously murdered at the instance of his ally Morcant, the British King of Northumberland, whilst preparing for battle against the Angles of Bernicia at Aber Lleu (the Low Estuary) near Metcaud (Lindisfarne) in 590. Urien was succeeded by his son Owain, who continued to protect Rheged from the onslaught of the Angles, heavily defeating Aethelric of Bernicia in 593. Although reliable documentation is rare for this period, it would appear that the British kings ruled for some two hundred years after the Romans left, bringing together the local Celtic tribes into a degree of unity which was essential if they were to protect themselves against the marauding bands of Picts and Dalriada Scots and overcome the constant threat of annexation by the Angles from across the Pennines. It was probably during this period that the hill fort on Allen Knott was renewed for active service. Although the fortification may well have been in existence before Roman times, it was almost certainly used to defend the local Celtic peoples against attack during the turbulent age of Rheged. Only a little more than a mile away to the east can be found the remains of a Celtic farming community dating from this same hostile period. The settlement – often referred to as the 'Hugill British Settlement' – is marked today by an irregular pattern of low, grassy ridges occupying a small field high up on the southern flank of Capple Howe overlooking the Gowan valley. Within this gently sloping area several small platforms, formerly occupied by huts, can be made out on the ground, and numerous heaps of stones mark the sites of Celtic dwellings.

These ancient huts would have been substantially constructed out of local stone, with low, circular walls including an overlap at the entrance, which formed a small porch to keep out the cold winds. The frame of the roof consisted of long wooden poles lashed together where they met at a point, and supported over the centre of the hut by a single upright post. The roof itself would have been thatched to keep out the rain, while the gaps between the dry-stone walling were filled with earth to keep out any draughts. Within the huts the air was dark, dank and suffocating, as the only outlet for smoke from the fire was through the thatch of the roof. The Britannic Celts lived in an uncomfortable and insanitary environment, and disease must have been rife in these crowded conditions. Yet the community continued to live successfully together for centuries, firm in the knowledge that they were able to band together and protect themselves from outside attack. The whole village was surrounded by a low mound capped by a wall, and the extensive view eastwards towards Staveley and southwards to School Knott ensured that the occupants would receive good warning of invaders coming from that direction.

The Celtic farming communities of the Windermere area continued to live under the protection of the kingdom of Rheged for over two centuries, making few changes to the area but leaving their signature in the names which they gave to the hills and rivers and to other notable features of the landscape. These Celtic names have remained largely intact to the present day and form the oldest group of place-names which have been handed down over the centuries from generation to generation. The Rivers Kent and Leven were given their names by these early Britons, as was the River Winster – the 'white stream' – which has since given its title to the neighbouring village. Towering above the valley floors, the mountain peaks of Helvellyn, Blencathra and Skiddaw were also christened at this time by our Celtic forefathers. While some of these Celtic names – like 'Cumbria' itself – are currently enjoying a new prominence in the local vocabulary, many of the Celtic names – such as 'Merin Rheged', the Solway Firth – dropped out of use long ago and have been all but lost to posterity.

It is also due to the evidence of place-names that we can be certain of a further threat which faced the local Celtic farmers of the Windermere area during the reign of the princes of Rheged. Even during the third century, before the withdrawal of the Roman legions from Britain, the south-east coastlands were experiencing raids from across the North Sea. After the Romans left, these attacks by Germanic pirates increased in frequency until their ravages could be tolerated no longer by the native Britons. The Venerable Bede recorded that in 449 these Angle and Saxon invaders were granted lands in East Anglia by King Vortigern, on condition that they protected the native Britons from the attacks of the Picts to the north. But once they arrived, the Anglo-Saxons allied themselves with the Picts and proceeded to conquer the whole of Lowland Britain. By the early seventh century the Angles of the Northumbrian kingdom were already pushing across the Pennines over Stainmore and through the

Tyne Gap. Place-names ending in 'ham' and 'ton' indicate the spread of Anglo-Saxon settlement across the Cumberland coastal plain from Wig*ton* to Working*ton* and on to Whic*ham* at the mouth of the Duddon valley. Dal*ton* and Penning*ton* in Low Furness were also settled by the Anglians at this time, and the colonization of the fertile lowlands of the lower Kent valley threw an almost complete circle of Northumbrian settlement around the uplands of the Central Lake District.

But while there is widespread evidence of Anglian settlement on the lowlands south of the Windermere area, stretching from Col*ton* and New*ton* to Hevers*ham* and Helsing*ton*, there is little evidence to suggest that the Anglian settlers penetrated the Windermere area itself. Indeed, with the possible exception of Res*ton* – which belongs more to the Kent valley than to the Windermere fells – the only Anglian place-names found in the Windermere area denote topographical features rather than village settlements. It is almost as if the Angles sailed up Windermere noting the lakeside ridge (Loughrigg), the lake with grassy shores (Grasmere) and even the bull-shaped headland (Bowness) but failed to plant any permanent settlement on its shores. This lack of Anglian settlement may have been due to the fierce resistance of the Celtic inhabitants, or perhaps it can be explained by a deliberate agreement to keep away from the poorer farming country of the Silurian foothills and the marshy floors of the Winster and Gilpin valleys. Whatever the reason, the Windermere area remained free of Anglian colonization and continued to remain in the hands of the Celtic peoples who had settled in the area long before the Romans arrived.

Although the Anglian settlement never spread deeply into the Lake District territory of the kingdom of Rheged, it was nevertheless as a direct result of the Anglian advance that this kingdom was finally brought close to collapse at the beginning of the seventh century. Bede records that, after the death of King Urien, Aethelfrith – the Anglian King of Bernicia – ravaged the Britons so successfully that even Aedun, King of the Dalriada Scots, was defeated in 603 when he came to their assistance at the Battle of Degsa's Stone. The end of Rheged as an independent kingdom was precipitated by a political marriage in c.638 when Riemmelth – the great-granddaughter of King Urien of Rheged – was married to Oswiu, brother of the Northumbrian King Oswald. This secured the Northumbrian hold on the territory from the Kent to the Clyde, and the whole of Cumbria became part of the Anglian kingdom of Northumbria.

Despite these political changes, the Windermere area continued to be inhabited by the same native Celtic farmers who had lived there for centuries, and the nominal presence of Anglian overlords had little effect on the local way of life. Celtic traditions and practices lived on throughout the seventh and eighth centuries, and as the Northumbrian influence west of the Pennines gradually declined during the ninth century, the old British kingdom of Strathclyde – centred on Dumbarton – regained much of the Celtic lands to the south. By c.900 Cumbria had been annexed to Strathclyde, and the two names were used synonymously during the tenth century. This Celtic kingdom of Strathclyde was the ruling force when yet another wave of invaders – the Norsemen – began to threaten the Celtic domination of the Windermere area in the early years of the tenth century.

5

Norse and Normans

The colonization of the Windermere area by people of Norse descent at the beginning of the tenth century was just a small part of the vast settlement programme which took these Scandinavian travellers to new homelands as far afield as Ireland, Greenland and North America. Large areas of Arctic waste which are today covered by permanent ice sheets, or by barren tundra, were settled at this time in the wake of Norwegian explorers who set out across the northern seas in their Viking longboats. During the early part of the ninth century scores of Norsemen set sail from the Norwegian fjords in a great westwards migration which brought the Scandinavian civilization to the nearly deserted shores of the Orkney and Shetland Isles. By the middle of the ninth century the southern coast of Iceland had been colonized by thousands of Norse farmers and had become a thriving Viking kingdom, sending out further waves of settlers to new lands beyond the seas. In c.985 some four hundred Norse Icelanders set sail for Greenland under the leadership of Erik the Red, and within two hundred years there were over four hundred farmsteads on the lush, green coastal pastures of south-west Greenland. The discovery of archaeological remains – including a spindle-whorl undoubtedly of Norse origin – at L'Anse aux Meadows on the northern coast of Newfoundland has confirmed that it was Norsemen who sailed on at this time to discover the north-east coast of America. At about the same time the Norse settlers of Shetland and Orkney were migrating further west along the north coast of Scotland, and by the end of the ninth century powerful Viking kingdoms had been established in the Western Isles, in the Isle of Man and on the coastal fringes of Ireland.

That these settlements – especially those in Iceland and Greenland – were at all possible was due, in large measure, to the milder climate which dominated the whole of north-west Europe from the ninth century to the thirteenth century. Recent analysis of the amount of heavy oxygen found in snow cores drilled in south-west Greenland has confirmed that the summer temperatures at that time were much higher than at present, allowing a longer growing season and resulting in much less pack ice to hinder navigation in the coastal waters. In England the Domesday survey, completed in 1086, records no less than thirty-eight vineyards in the South of England, and it was quite possible to grow soft fruits such as peaches and apricots in the North of England at that time. It was during this warmer climatic phase that the glaciers retreated from the coasts of Iceland and Greenland, and Norse settlements became feasible in areas which are now beyond permanent human habitation. This amelioration of the climate also made the uplands of the Central Lake District far more hospitable for inhabitation than they are today.

There is no contemporary evidence to tell us when the first Scandinavian settlers arrived in the Windermere area, but we know that the coast further south was colonized at the beginning of the tenth century. Perhaps as a result of overcrowding, the Viking warrior Ingermund and his followers were expelled from the Norse kingdom of Dublin in 901 or 902, and were given lands to settle near Chester by Aethelfled, the Lady of the Mercians. Further settlements along the coast of Lancashire and Cumbria probably took place shortly afterwards, and by the end of the tenth century even the remotest valleys of Central Lakeland had been colonized by these Norse-Irish farmers. Windermere – literally 'Vinand's lake' – became an artery of Norse trade, and the valley floor and foothills – previously the home of scattered Celtic tribes – became quite densely populated with the homesteads of Norse farmers.

While the tenth-century colonization was interspersed with hostile Norse-Irish raids which devastated Carlisle on more than one occasion and forced the Abbot of Heversham to retreat across the Pennines, on the whole the settlement was largely peaceful. During the early years of colonization the Norsemen either purchased land from the small native Celtic community or else moved onto land – especially upland pastures – which had not previously been utilized. There was little opposition from the native residents, and in time the tall, fair-haired Scandinavians and the short, stocky, dark-haired Celts intermarried to produce the mixed ancestry of today's farmers.

When the Norse first arrived, Windermere was part of the sparsely populated Celtic kingdom of Strathclyde ruled by King Owain before the Battle of Brunanburh in 936, and then by King Dunmail. Dunmail ruled until 945 when the Anglo-Saxon Chronicle tells us that Edmund, King of the Saxons, defeated and deposed him, handing over the whole of Cumbria to his own ally Malcolm, King of the Scots. From c.940 the Norse were, for the most part, allies of the Scots, and the settlement proceeded relatively peacefully after the Windermere area became part of Scotland in 945.

The vast majority of settlements in the Windermere area date from this period of Norse migration, and the individual place-names tell us much about the nature of the colonization and the way of life of these Scandinavian settlers. The Norse farmers were predominantly pastoralists and relied for their prosperity on extensive flocks of sheep, with smaller numbers of cattle, pigs and goats, and patches of arable land near the homesteads. The wooded lowlands of the Windermere valley provided potentially rich pastures, and once again the lake-bed sediments faithfully provide the evidence that the Norse settlers quickly cleared extensive tracts of woodland to provide grazing for their animals. Local place-names also confirm the disappearance of the trees, with the Scandinavian element *thveit* or *thwaite* indicating a clearing in the woodland. Typical of these early Norse settlements was Finsthwaite, which began its existence as 'Finn's clearing', while Heathwaite, near Windermere village, had its origins as 'the high clearing'. Birthwaite – the name of the hamlet where Windermere village now stands – indicates a clearing in the birch woodland, while Esthwaite Water was the lake beside the clearing in the ash trees, and Applethwaite was the clearing with the apple tree.

While much of the local woodland was cleared to provide pasture for sheep, some place-names identify local pockets of land which were cleared for the cultivation of arable crops. Thus Rydal was the name given to the valley where rye was grown, while Haverthwaite – on the floor of the Leven valley – indicates a clearing where oats were cultivated. Sometimes the trees were not felled but were used as pannage for swine. In the oak woodlands of Grizedale many hundreds of pigs – *griss* in Norse – would have been content to snuffle for acorns among the wooded knolls at the head of the valley.

The damper lowland pastures, where grass would have grown most rapidly, were too damp for sheep to graze, and here cattle would have been kept. The name '*ings*' denotes a well-watered meadow, and the land on the floor of the Gowan valley surrounding the hamlet of Ings matches this description perfectly. The Norse farmers were well aware of the dangers of overgrazing, and in order to combat this problem the use of each acre of pasture was carefully regulated. An allocated minimum allowance of grazing was designated a '*stint*', and the animals would be given a controlled *stint* in each area of pasture or '*grass*'. One *grass* – covering approximately eight acres – was regarded as sufficient permanent pasture to graze a horse and a colt, three cows, seventeen sheep and twenty geese. The manure from the horses and cattle would ensure that the pasture was not exhausted by the constant grazing, while all together the animals would provide meat, eggs, milk and wool for clothing. A small farm, or '*garth*', would need eight or ten *grasses* – some eighty acres of permanent pasture within easy reach of the farmstead.

The settlement at Grassgarth, near Ings, dates from the tenth century, when the *stint* was strictly operated on the *ings* and *grasses* of the Gowan valley. While the animals were grazed on the *grassgarth* or in-fields during the winter months, over the summer the sheep and cattle were fed on the common pastures or out-fields high up on the open fells. During late spring the young men and women would drive the herds up to the summer pasture or *saeter*, returning before the winter set in with a supply of cheese and butter which had been prepared from the summer's milk. This process of transhumance or *saeterbruk* ensured that the in-fields were not constantly grazed during the drier summer season and allowed the farmers to lay in a fair crop of hay ready for the winter feed.

A number of these summer farms or *saeters* have today grown into quite sizeable settlements. Ambleside – which appears in its earlier form as 'Amelsate' in a manuscript of 1274 – probably had its origins as 'Hamel's *saeter*'; while Hawkshead – referred to in a twelfth-century document as 'Houkesete' – was undoubtedly the summer farmstead belonging to Houkr. Similarly, Satterthwaite, in the Grizedale valley, identified 'the *saeter* in the clearing', while other local Norse place-names reveal the summer pastures on the fells surrounding Windermere. Latterbarrow, for example, indicated 'the hill where animals live', while Sweden Crag overlooked the *swithin* or moorland pasture cleared by burning.

While many settlements originally founded in Norse times can still be identified by their original Scandinavian place-names, there are, however, few *visible* remains of the actual buildings erected by the Norse farmers themselves. In most cases, these early dwelling sites have been totally obliterated by subsequent development, but in the upper Troutbeck valley, on the west side of Troutbeck Tongue, there can still be found the remains of a number of Norse-Irish huts. These huts were probably temporary *shielings* – the dwellings used on the *saeter* during the summer season. They are nevertheless substantially built of dry-stone walling and would formerly have been thatched with turf and floored with bracken, freshly collected from the fells.

The most extensive legacy of Norse place-names refer, however, not to the numerous homesteads where the Norsemen settled but to the countless topographical features such as rivers and streams, rocky summits and high waterfalls which tumble down the steep valley-sides. Numerous 'becks' and 'gills' flow into the rivers of Lakeland, while 'barrows' and 'knotts' rise high above the valley floors, and watery 'forces' cascade down their steep slopes. The Trout Beck – which appears in a document of 1292 as 'Trutebyk' – owes its name to the Norse settlers, while Black Beck – the former boundary between Lancashire and Westmorland first recorded in 1170 – also dates back to Viking times. Other topographical features include Hugill, refering to a high ravine, and Claife, which signifies the steep, cliff-like slope on the western side of the Windermere valley. Similarly,

Skelwith identifies 'the ford near the noisy one' – a reference, no doubt, to the nearby waterfall at Skelwith Force, while Capplebarrow indicates the *kapall beorg* – the nag's hill. The many islands rising from the waters of Windermere itself were called *holmr* by the Norsemen. Rough Holme and Grass Holme have retained their titles to the present day, while Belle Isle – known for centuries as Long Holme – was re-named in 1781 by its new owner, Isabella Curwen.

Many other Scandinavian names occur in the Windermere area and throughout the Furness district. A quick glance at a local map will reveal numerous examples of Norse place-names such as *slack* (a valley), *howe* (a hill), *wray* (a remote place), *with* (a wood), *dub* (a tarn), *ees* (an island), *pull* (a pool) and *wyke* (a bay). Furness itself refers to 'the headland with an island', but another prominent local place-name cannot be explained so easily. Orrest Head derives its name from the Old Norse *orrosta* meaning 'a battle'. But if Orrest Head was indeed the site of a battle during the tenth century, then it is uncertain which encounter the name refers to. Does it refer to the battle of 945 when Edmund defeated Dunmail and assigned the whole of Cumbria to Malcolm, King of the Scots? Might it be associated with the ravages of Earl Thored who harried Westmorland in 966? Or does it refer to the campaign of the year 1000 when, the Anglo-Saxon Chronicle tells us, 'This year the King [Ethelred] went into Cumberland, and nearly laid waste the whole of it with his army'? Whatever the date and ultimate outcome of the Orrest Head battle, the whole of the Lake District remained part of Scotland during the Norse settlement, and only in 1032, when King Canute handed over Lothian to the Scots in exchange for Cumbria, was the national boundary that we know today created for the first time.

If we pause to consider the large number of villages and towns in the Windermere area which still retain their original Norse place-names, we might be tempted to imagine that by the end of the tenth century the area was densely populated with numerous sizeable settlements. Yet we must constantly bear in mind that each of these settlements has grown to its present size from very small beginnings. While the Anglo-Saxons with their arable system of farming – requiring the use of a communal plough and plough team – had always settled in villages, the Norse, with their dominantly pastoral system, invariably settled in isolated farmsteads or hamlets. The need for extensive grazing land in close proximity to each farmstead demanded that the settlements be well spaced and mitigated against the larger villages common throughout lowland England. Consequently, even though the area surrounding Windermere became densely filled with Scandinavian place-names during the Norse settlement, there were no real villages in the area, and even at the end of the tenth century the area still contained only a relatively sparse (though well-distributed) population.

Undoubtedly the major impact that the Norse settlement had on the Windermere area was not the appearance of large settlements in the landscape but the extensive clearing of the woodlands on the slopes of the surrounding fells. Pollen analysis of sediment cores taken from the bed of Ellerside Moss, south of Haverthwaite, has confirmed that during the Norse settlement the amount of oak pollen declined while the amount of pollen from grasses, heather and bracken increased rapidly. By the time of the Domesday survey, in 1086, the fellsides of the Windermere area were almost certainly far less wooded than they are today, due to the clearance of large areas for pasture during the Norse settlement (and following the subsequent reafforestation which has occurred since the seventeenth century).

While this extensive clearance of the woodlands can be accepted without any reasonable doubt, it is impossible to verify this picture of the Windermere landscape from the record of the Domesday Book itself. When William of Normandy despatched his messengers to all parts of the country in 1086, in order to assess the wealth of his kingdom, some twenty years had elapsed since the defeat of the Saxons at Senlac Hill, yet William had not, during that time, been able to secure a firm hold on the northern border regions of his kingdom. At the time of William's invasion, Malcolm III – King of the Scots and ally of the defeated Saxons – had taken the opportunity to cross the Solway and had annexed the whole of the central and northern parts of the Lake District. At the time of the Domesday Survey, the whole of Cumberland and the northern half of Westmorland lay, once again, under the jurisdiction of the Scottish Crown. Windermere itself, after the Norman Conquest, formed the western boundary of the manor of Kendal, held in 1086 by Gilemichel, a landowner of Norse-Irish descent. But while Low Furness and other parts of Lancashire north of the Ribble appear in the Domesday Book (as part of the Amounderness district of Yorkshire), the Furness Fells were very much part of the disputed border region at this time and do not figure in the Domesday accounts.

As a result, it is impossible to confirm – from written sources – the appearance of the landscape with any accuracy, but it is safe to say that, in its early years, the Norman Conquest made little impact on the Windermere landscape. The life of the local Anglo-Norse population went on unchanged despite the political struggles between the kingdoms of England and Scotland. As late as the mid-twelfth century, Norse continued to be the spoken language of the local population, and the area continued to be a border region sparsely populated by Norse sheep farmers throughout the political upheavals of the eleventh century.

In the years immediately preceding the Domesday survey, King William had nevertheless made a determined effort to wrest the northern part of Saxon England from the Scots. In 1072 William sailed up the east coast with his army, landed by the Tay and attacked Malcolm III, who was forced – for the time being – to retreat northwards. But the peace was short-lived, and in 1079 the Scots moved south again, plundering Northumberland as far south as the Tyne. In the west, the political situation remained equally unsettled until after William's death. A more decisive outcome was achieved by William II, who, in answer to a raid by the Scots, marched north to Carlisle in 1092, drove out Dolfin, the Earl of Northumberland, and occupied the castle. The following year Malcolm III was killed while invading England, and his successor – his brother Dufnal – was deposed by an English army in 1097 and replaced first by Malcolm's son Duncan (who was almost immediately murdered) and then by another son, Edgar, who had been brought up at the English Court.

After 1092 William completely re-organized the defence of the northern marchlands, establishing a vast colony of frontier settlers on the surrounding lands and placing the defence of the border region in the hands of powerful Norman barons. Carlisle was established as the frontier stronghold of the barony of Carlisle, while the baronies of Copeland and Appleby were intended to act as a second line of defence. Further south, the barony of Kendal – stretching from the Lune valley to Windermere – was given to Yvo Talboise, and Furness was granted to Roger, Count of Poitou, who also held much of the area of Lancashire south of the sands. The Cartmel peninsula, on the other hand, remained in the hands of the Crown until 1186 when the area was granted to William, Earl of Pembroke and Grand Marshal of England. In 1120 the baronies of Carlisle, Appleby and Kendal came into the possession of the Crown, and Henry I once again re-organized the border area by creating the counties of Cumberland and Westmorland under shire-reeves, or sheriffs. As a result, William II and Henry I after him were able to secure their hold on the Lake District far more effectively than William I, and despite the many Scottish raids during the twelfth and thirteenth centuries, the balance of power in the Windermere area remained decisively in English hands after 1092.

Meanwhile, in c.1114, Stephen of Blois, Count of Boulogne and nephew of Henry I, had received from his uncle a grant of land including the territories of Furness and Cartmel. In 1123 Stephen gave a small area of land, at Tulketh near Preston, for the establishment of a monastic house by monks of the Order of Savigny – an order recently founded in Normandy. Four years later, in 1127, Stephen granted this foundation a more extensive parcel of land, covering much of the Furness peninsula and the fells of High Furness, and the monks subsequently moved to a remote valley – known locally as 'the Valley of the Deadly Nightshade' – some two miles inland from the coast near Walney Island. By the time of the suppression of the monasteries in 1537, Furness Abbey had become the wealthiest and most powerful monastic house in the Lake District, and during the four centuries of its existence the monks of Furness were to have a far greater effect on the landscape of the Windermere area than any other previous settlers who had arrived on its shores.

6

Furness Abbey and Medieval Industries

When the Savignac monks of Preston moved their few possessions to the Furness peninsula in 1127, their immediate presence must have gone largely unnoticed by the Norse-Irish farmers who still pastured their scattered flocks among the fells of High Furness on the western shores of Windermere. Yet within a few years these new landlords were to have a profound effect not only on the lives of the local populace but also on the appearance of the Furness Fells themselves. Some twenty years later, in 1147, the monastic order of Savigny and the order of Cîteaux were amalgamated, and the monks of Furness found themselves – somewhat unwillingly – absorbed into the great Cistercian movement. The Cistercian order was perhaps the most outstanding of the great revivals within the Benedictine order, and it was as a Cistercian house that Furness rose to become the most powerful of all the Lake District monastic communities.

When the monks of Furness Abbey had been granted their new lands by Stephen of Blois, at the beginning of the twelfth century, the southern fells of the Lake District were still very much part of an unknown and disputed border region, and the precise extent of the estate was uncertain. In addition to the low-lying Furness peninsula itself, the abbey lands included the greater part of the fell country lying further north between the Duddon and the Leven valleys. The exact boundaries of this hill country were not, however, clearly defined and when, in c.1150, the first William of Lancaster received a large grant of land from Roger de Mowbray – including the neighbouring lands of

Lonsdale and Kentdale – he immediately laid claim to the disputed area of the Furness Fells to the west of Windermere. Collingwood, in his *Lake District History*, recounts how the local residents settled the dispute:

> Thirty sworn men beat the boundaries and enclosed the fells with a line taken from Wrynose down the Duddon on the West and down the Brathay and Windermere on the East. They halved this block by following Yewdale Beck, Coniston Water and the River Crake. William de Lancaster chose the western half, leaving Hawkshead, Satterthwaite and Colton to the Abbey. This was ratified by Henry II in c.1163.

As a result of this agreement, Windermere became the eastern boundary of the abbey lands, which stretched beyond the Grizedale valley to the shores of Coniston Water, while on the northern and eastern shores of Windermere the de Lancasters were to hold the barony of Kendal for many generations to come. To the south-east the lowlands of the Cartmel peninsula and the fell country bordering the southern shores of Windermere soon came under the influence of the Augustinian friars of Cartmel Priory, founded as a daughter house of Carlisle Priory some sixty years after the foundation of Furness Abbey. The friars were given the low-lying lands of the Cartmel peninsula and the hill country of Cartmel Fell in 1188 by William Marshall, Earl of Pembroke, and thereby became the second religious house to be granted land on the shores of Windermere. This threefold division of the land bordering Windermere remained virtually intact for over eight hundred years as Furness and Cartmel were amalgamated into Lancashire, North of the Sands, while the baronies of Kendal and Appleby were subsequently joined to form the county of Westmorland. Only with the creation of the new county of Cumbria, in the administrative reforms of 1974, did these three neighbouring areas come under one authority.

Of all the lands owned by Furness Abbey, undoubtedly its most valuable possession was the manor of Hawkshead. Originally founded in the eleventh century by Norse-Irish settlers, the tiny village of Hawkshead was rapidly transformed into a thriving commercial centre as the abbey increased its wealth. In order to establish his control over the territory between Windermere and Coniston Water, the abbot of Furness established a grange, or abbey farm, at Hawkshead in the early thirteenth century. From this monastic grange the abbot, on his regular visits to the area, controlled the affairs of the local population, dispensing justice at the manorial court and collecting the local tithes in due season. Hawkshead Hall – a sixteenth-century farmhouse – was built on the site of the abbey grange, obliterating all the earlier buildings belonging to the abbey. Fortunately, the fifteenth-century gatehouse – which includes the old manorial court house, built over the arch – was incorporated into the farm buildings and is now under the guardianship of the National Trust. Up to the time of the dissolution, the abbey controlled every aspect of the life of the local population. The abbey church, built on a small rise and dominating the village, served originally as a private chapel for the monks, but in 1219 its doors were opened to all, and it subsequently became the parish church of Hawkshead when the larger parish of Dalton was sub-divided in 1578. Other facilities which the local residents were obliged to use included the manorial cornmill, situated close by the grange farm and still in use as late as the nineteenth century.

In common with other Cistercian houses in England, the wealth of Furness Abbey was founded on the wool trade. The Cistercians or 'White Monks' – so called because of their white woollen habits – belonged to an order which emphasized the spiritual and mental benefits of manual labour, rather than encouraging a dedication to learning and scholarship. Not surprisingly, perhaps, their motto – 'To work is to pray' – also ensured that the house was blessed with considerable wealth and financial success. Monastic life, nevertheless, was uncompromisingly simple, with only the basic necessities such as food and warm woollen clothing provided for the material needs of the fraternity. Luxuries were few and far between; in accordance with their strict rule, the monks were allowed the comfort of an open fire only once a year, on Christmas Day, and when they were sick. As a result of their own labours, the brothers were largely self-sufficient in foodstuffs. The monastic house grew its own barley and brewed its own beer, and the monks kept sheep for their own use – to supply the wool needed for their thick woollen habits.

Based on a firm foundation of Christian piety and hard work, the Cistercians soon became excellent sheep farmers and, assisted by generous benefactors, rapidly acquired huge flocks and extensive pastures. The short, tough wool of the local hill sheep was in great demand on the Continent, and much of the wool produced on the Furness Fells was sold by the abbey to meet the cost of stonemasons and craftsmen employed in the construction of the splendid monastic buildings whose remains can still be seen today. By 1292 Furness Abbey owned fourteen granges as far afield as High Furness, Eskdale and Borrowdale, and each year fifteen thousand sheep were wintered on Walney Island. As only the young breeding ewes would have been brought down to the coast in winter, the total number of sheep held by the abbey must have exceeded sixty or seventy thousand.

It was also around this time that a marked change in the climate of Britain encouraged the expansion of the woollen industry. During the Norse colonization of the Windermere area in the tenth century, the climate of the region was much warmer than at the present day, and it continued to remain mild throughout the following century, reaching a climatic optimum between 1170 and 1200. But with the coming of the thirteenth century the weather rapidly began to deteriorate. Although there are no local climatic records dating from this period, we can gauge the extent of this deterioration from the accounts of contemporary travellers. The Icelandic Sagas, for example, written shortly after 1200, noted the first appearance of Arctic drift ice in the Denmark Strait between Iceland and Greenland, and by the end of the century the advancing ice floes were regularly proving a navigational hazard to ships crossing the North Atlantic from Europe to Greenland. Isotope studies of cores taken from the Greenland ice-cap have confirmed that by 1300 the climate had become both colder and drier than today. This climatic pattern was repeated throughout Western Europe, and by the end of the thirteenth century the demand for warmer, thicker clothes had already led to an upsurge of activity in the medieval woollen industry.

To meet this demand for heavy woollen clothing, large areas of northern England, often in the hands of monastic communities, were transformed from barren moorlands into extensive and profitable sheep-runs. On the Furness Fells above the western shores of Windermere, the monks of Furness Abbey created a number of new farms from the waste land during the fourteenth century. Unlike the earlier Norse settlers who had established their *saeters* on the sheltered valley floors at Satterthwaite, Finsthwaite and Hawkshead, the monks built their new farmsteads on remote, upland sites. The new settlements were perched high up on the slopes of the fells, where the rough upland pastures provided extensive grazing for their rapidly expanding flocks. The Coucher Book of Furness Abbey records that the establishment of these new monastic grange farms was authorized in 1338 when Edward III granted the abbot a licence to enclose land from the waste 'at Clayf and Furness Fells'. The arduous task of clearing the land and establishing these new farms, however, did not necessarily fall upon the monks themselves. While the abbey acted as landlord and was the driving force behind the scheme, the fells were often reclaimed by lay brothers or by local tenants of the abbey who supplied vast quantities of wool and various essential foodstuffs to the abbey in payment of their ground rent.

These remote, scattered farms can be identified today by their name, which includes the word 'Park' – a name introduced by the Normans to signify a piece of land enclosed for pasture or for arable farming. Lawson Park and Parkamoor, high up on the steep slopes overlooking Coniston Water, typify the isolation of these monastic farmsteads, while Abbot Park, Hill Park and Oxen Park, north of Colton, and Dale Park and Stott Park, between Windermere and Grizedale, were all colonized at this time. Abbots Reading, north of Haverthwaite, is also the site of a medieval grange farm established by the monks of Furness Abbey during the fourteenth century.

The effect that the enclosure of these vast areas of upland had on the local vegetation was profound. Although, probably, only a small amount of the woodland was deliberately cleared for pasture, the long-term effect of constant grazing was much more far-reaching. As the sheep continually destroyed the young seedlings in their endless search for food, the woodlands were

Common Farm, Applethwaite—a 'statesman's' house

Seventeenth-century 'statesman's' houses at High Green, Troutbeck

Fusethwaite Yeat, near Troutbeck—a seventeenth-century yeoman's house

Gill Head, Cartmel Fell, built in 1719 for a yeoman farmer

The Bridge House, Ambleside—a summerhouse of Ambleside Hall

Braithwaite's corn mill at 'Rattle Gill', Ambleside

Low Millerground, where the bell used to call the ferry from Belle Grange

Thompson Ground, Hawkshead—a seventeenth-century 'longhouse'

A seventeenth-century 'statesman's' barn, Troutbeck

Remains of the ironworks at Backbarrow

The first blast furnace in the North of England, constructed at Backbarrow in 1711

Stott Park bobbin mill, Finsthwaite

High Dam, Finsthwaite Heights

The Round House on
Belle Isle, built in 1774
by John Plaw

unable to regenerate, and in time the extensive tree cover was reduced to a few isolated stands amongst a tangle of rough grassland. The constant deforestation of the Furness Fells from the thirteenth to the seventeenth century has again been confirmed by the analysis of pollen in cores which have been retrieved from a number of local tarns and peat bogs. Pollen counts on these samples invariably reflect a marked decrease in timber and a sharp increase in grasses during the medieval period. By the time of the Dissolution of the Monasteries in 1537, much of High Furness had become a vast sheep-run, and some areas on the western shore of Windermere were almost devoid of trees – a picture very different from the situation today.

The woodlands of the western shore, however, were not the only ones to be affected by clearance during the twelfth and thirteenth centuries. To the east of Windermere the lands belonging to the barony of Kendal had for many years been preserved in their natural state as a hunting forest. Yet a letter sent from Henry III to the third William de Lancaster in 1225 shows that during the thirteenth century the lands of the Kendal barony were slowly being reclaimed for pasture and arable farming. In his letter the King rebuked William for preventing certain 'knights and true men' from clearing and reclaiming areas of the forest, 'whereas we granted and commanded that all the woods, except our own demesne woods, should be disafforested ... and you, nevertheless, hold as forest in the same state as they formerly were certain woodlands and moors, to the injury and loss of your true men and neighbours.' Large numbers of sheep were being reared at this time on the moorland pastures of Applethwaite Common and the Troutbeck Hundreds, and once again it was largely local tenants who were finding that the breeding of sheep on these former waste lands could prove to be a very remunerative trade.

By the end of the thirteenth century wool had become Britain's most important export to the Continent, and the woolsack had become the financial symbol of the English Exchequer. Many hundreds of woolsacks passed annually through Kendal *en route* to the south-coast Channel ports, while Furness Abbey sent about thirty woolsacks annually to Italy alone. A woolsack consisted of a hundred fleeces tightly bound together, and at 18½ marks per sack the high-quality short-woolled fleeces from the Lake District brought a higher than average price. All English wool had to be exported through the Staple, established by Edward I as a source of taxation. In 1261 Furness Abbey had applied for special concessions and had been given 'quit of all wool taxes and tolls, and charges for transport and transit' and permission to land wool at the small port of Wissant, twelve miles west of Calais. But in 1423 the merchants of the Calais Staple insisted that these generous concessions be cast aside, and the abbot of Furness was heavily fined for shipping a load of four hundred 'sarplers' (large sacks of wool) from 'le Peele de Foddray' (Piel Island, near Barrow).

Most of the wool for export was carried by packhorse to the south coast of England, from where it was shipped, via the Staple, to Flanders. Italian merchants, however, were given special concessions. As well as being able to export wool independently of the Staple, they were also allowed to travel throughout England in search of supplies. As a result, Furness Abbey, together with the monastic houses at Shap, Calder and Holme Cultrum, traded directly with the Italian merchants, and on these journeys the Italians were able to buy 'futures' – the fleeces which would be shorn in the forthcoming season.

While raw wool continued to be in great demand on the Continent throughout medieval times, from the thirteenth century onwards more and more English wool began to be exported by the Merchant Adventurers in the form of woollen cloth. The woollen industry was a domestic or cottage industry, and each member of the family played his or her part in the production of the finished cloth.

The first process, usually carried out by the tenant's wife, involved the carding of the wool, using hand combs made of teazles to make the fibres lie parallel. Next the spinster daughters spun the woollen fibres into yarn, often working outside with their distaffs or sitting in the spinning gallery – several later versions of which can still be seen amongst the farmhouses of the Troutbeck valley. The yarn was woven into cloth by the men, who worked in their cottages on small hand looms. Before dyeing in birch bark or dyers' greenweed, the cloth was boiled, to remove the natural greases, in a vat containing potash soap. The soap was prepared locally in a potash kiln, the potash being produced by burning enormous amounts of bracken from the local fellsides or 'brackenriggs'. A series of at least five of these potash kilns lies on the west side of the Troutbeck valley near Longmire Yeat and Fusethwaite Yeat where the 'yeats' (gates), leading from the valley, open up onto the common pastures.

Next the cloth was taken to the fulling mill where the mill wheel drove the fulling stocks which hammered the cloth back into shape. The process of fulling had been mechanized on the Continent since the early part of the eleventh century, but it was not until the middle of the twelfth century that water-powered fulling mills began to appear in the Windermere area. One of these early mills was built at Troutbeck Bridge in 1274 and served as the communal fulling mill for the township of Applethwaite. As a carry-over from the earlier days of fulling by foot in a trough of soapy water, the rents paid for the use of the fulling mill were referred to as 'walking silver' in the Troutbeck area. Finally the finished cloth was washed in the stream and stretched out to dry on tenter hooks before being stacked ready for collection by the packmen.

Usually, as at Troutbeck, the fulling mill, brackenriggs, potash kilns and tenter fields were located in close proximity to each other. Such a pattern existed at Ambleside, where Stock Ghyll (known earlier as Sleddal Beck) provided power for the fulling stocks, and Stock Ghyll Mill (now converted into holiday flats) operated as the fulling mill for the township. Local bracken, for the manufacture of potash soap, was obtained from the brackenriggs on the slopes of Wansfell Pike, while at least three potash kilns were in use on the banks of Stock Ghyll, upstream from the mill. The old tenter field, where the finished cloth was hung out to dry, is now occupied by the Ambleside bus station. On the Furness Fells to the west of Windermere, fulling mills and potash kilns were again found in symbiosis. The Rental prepared by the commissioners at the dissolution of Furness Abbey in 1537 records two fulling mills in High Furness – one at Sawrey Extra (Far Sawrey) and the other at Hawkshead Hill. At the latter site, one of the cottages is still traditionally remembered as a weaver's home, while nearby at Tenter Hill the wet cloth was hung out to dry. Bracken once grew extensively on the slopes of High Furness, while no less than seventeen potash kilns have been identified on the western shores of Windermere between Newby Bridge and Hawkshead.

While the whole process of manufacturing woollen cloth could, if necessary, be performed by one family, cottagers usually worked for a local clothier as part of a large team. Wealthy clothiers, such as Thomas Jackson of Ambleside and John Benson of Loughrigg, each organized the employment of up to a hundred cottagers – arranging for the collection and sorting of the fleeces, the putting-out of the wool to spinsters and the redistribution of the finished yarn to the weavers. At each stage the wool was carried by packhorse, and the packmen were vital members of the team. The ancient 'Carrier's Arms', depicted in the stained glass of Windermere parish church, reminds us of the tools of the packman's trade – the packing pricks, the Wantey Hook and the rope, all essential items needed to secure a load of woolpacks as the packman led his horse southwards to Kendal.

Although wool formed the primary export of England during medieval times, it was not the only source of wealth from High Furness. While large patches of the fells were reclaimed for sheep pastures during the medieval period, huge areas of woodland still remained – especially on the steeper and more inaccessible slopes. Timber has always constituted an important resource in the Lake District, and as early as 1246 the fourth William de Lancaster granted Furness Abbey the right to launch 'two suitable boats, namely one on Windermere, and another on Thurstanswater [i.e. Coniston Water] to carry their wood and timber and whatever else they need'. At the dissolution of the abbey in 1537, the King's commissioners reported: '... there is moche wood growing in Furneysfells in the mounteynes there, [including] Byrk, Holey, Asshe, Ellers, Lyng, lytell short Okes, and other Undrewood ....' The report goes on to detail some of the ways in which the woodlands were used: 'Also there ys another yerely profytte commying and growing of the said Woodes, called Grenehewe, Bastyng, Blecking, byndying, making of Sadeltrees, Cartwheles, Cupes, Disshes, and many other thynges wrought by Cowpers and Turners, with making of Coles, and panage of Hogges.'

This celebrated list of woodland trades catalogues many of the age-old traditional rights of the abbey's tenants, as well as including some more recent occupations. 'Grenehewe', for instance, was the customary payment made by the tenants to the Lord of the Manor for the right to take wood for their own personal use. This traditional right was not confined to the monastic tenants on the western shores of Windermere, as the Court Rolls of 1442 show that the tenants of Applethwaite, Troutbeck and Ambleside also paid green-hew to the barony of Kendal. A further traditional right involved the use of the woodlands for grazing pigs, referred to here as 'panage of Hogges'. Apart from domestic matters, the wood was also used to make a wide variety of products. 'Bastyng' refers to the manufacture of a coarse matting, while 'blecking' involved the bleaching or dyeing of bark, possibly to produce the potash soap needed in the fulling process. 'Bynding' was the general term used to describe the making of barrels, baskets and hoops, while the products of coopers and turners included, amongst other things, 'Sadeltrees' – the strong wooden frames used for packsaddles, cartwheels and domestic utensils. Each of these products formed the basis of important woodland industries which continued to thrive for centuries after the dissolution of the abbey. To the rear of the manor house at Hawkshead Hall, the monks established a small sawmill powered by water where the stream had been blocked by a small dam. Here cartwheels, cups and dishes have been turned by hand for centuries, and although the mill has been used for various purposes since monastic times, the twentieth century has seen it being used once again as the premises of a joiner and wheelwright.

Perhaps the most important of all the medieval woodland industries – the 'making of Coles', or charcoal – was destined to a somewhat shorter life. During the fourteenth and fifteenth centuries, charcoal was an essential prerequisite for smelting local iron ores, and later, during Elizabethan times, charcoal was in heavy demand for refining lead and copper ores. The wood required for charcoal-making was skilfully chosen to ensure that it became charred throughout. Young sprigs of hazel, alder or birch – no thicker than the wrist – were painstakingly stacked end to end on the flat floor of the charcoal pitstead. The charcoal

burner carefully covered the mound of sticks with a layer of turf –
to exclude the air – before setting fire to the stack from within.
Whenever a jet of smoke began to billow out through a gap in the
turf, the charcoal burner would quickly heap a spadeful of earth
onto the spot in order to smother the flames.

The necessity for a constant watch to be kept on the mound
meant that the charcoal burner had to remain on the job both
day and night, and a temporary hut would be built to provide
some shelter from the cold. The charcoal burner's hut was
constructed by driving short wooden stakes into the ground to
form low walls, with a gap – sometimes covered by old sacking –
to act as a narrow entrance. The roof consisted of long, thin poles
laid side by side and lashed together where they overlapped at
the top, while any gaps were plugged with leaves or moss to keep
out the wind. Sometimes, for ease of construction, the upright
walls were omitted, and the roof poles reached all the way to the
ground, forming a conical hut somewhat resembling an Indian
tepee.

The charcoal was burned slowly for twenty-four hours before
the turf was removed and the smouldering ashes were raked
away. High-quality charcoal was a very valuable commodity,
and, in order to provide sufficient quantities of young timber,
many of the woodlands were coppiced every fifteen or twenty
years to provide new growth.

Charcoal produced in this way was used to smelt local iron in
small bloomsmithies situated in the woodlands on both sides of
the lake, near the sources of charcoal. In the early sixteenth
century iron-smelting sites are known to have existed at Matson
Ground, near Bowness, and at Fell Foot, near Staveley, while the
Commissioners' Report of 1537 tells us that 'the Abbots of the
same late Monastery have been accustomed to have a Smythey,
and sometimes two or three, kepte for making of Yron to those of
their Monastery.' Iron-making became a profitable sideline for
the monastic community, and traces of the abbey's bloomeries
can still be found near the eastern shores of Coniston Water.
After the dissolution, the woodlands were rented for £20 per
annum to William Sandes and John Sawrey to provide charcoal
for their three smithies. These small iron bloomeries were,
however, short-lived as in 1565 Queen Elizabeth, worried by the

wholesale destruction of England's woodlands, decreed a ban on charcoal-making for the purposes of iron-smelting.

Curiously, however, it was the extensive prospecting for minerals during Elizabeth's reign that led to the large-scale development of another associated woodland industry. In 1538, at a court at Colton, Thomas Rawlinson of Haverthwaite was convicted 'for cutting the woods without licence and using the art called *elying of asshes*'. The process of 'ealing' involved the production of 'white coles' or 'kilnwood' – a form of dried timber which burned at an even rate and was therefore suitable for smelting lead and copper ores. The 'white coles' were prepared in a large kiln some fifteen feet high and thirty feet wide, where a fire in the base drove off the moisture from the timber which was laid across the upper part of the kiln. The largest kilns of this type in High Furness were located at Graythwaite and at Ealinghearth in the Rusland Valley, where in 1547 Myles and William Sawrey were permitted 'to make two little houses and hearths called *Ealing-hearths* on their tenements in Furnessfells, Co. Lancs & to take broken wood and sticks ther & on all other men's farm holds in Furnessfells for the term of 21 years paying 40s a year'.

The preparation of 'white coles' proceeded hand-in-hand with the pioneering mining operations of the Company of the Mines Royal, founded by Queen Elizabeth in 1564. Having discovered copper and lead ores at Goldscope and Newlands, on the western shores of Derwent Water, the German miners shipped the ores across the lake to the Greta valley, where they were smelted at the Brigham smelter near Keswick. In 1570 a royal decree highlighted the urgent need for fuel at the Brigham smelter, and as a result 'six hundred seme of coles [were] to be delyv'ed to the quenes Mats use nere the water of Wenndermyre at a reasonable p'ce'. The 'white coles' came from kilns as far afield as Graythwaite and Satterthwaite and included eleven kilns lying close to the shores of Windermere – nine on the west bank between Canny Hill and Blelham Tarn, and two on the east bank, at Holbeck Ghyll near Low Wood, and in Rayrigg Woods near Bowness. Another large kiln of this type can be located beside the stream at Elfhow in the Kentmere valley and remains almost intact to the present day.

While the production of 'white coles' remained a thriving trade for more than a hundred years, the end of the industry came during the Civil War, in 1648, when the Keswick smelter was destroyed by a force of Parliamentarians.

One further use of the woodlands has left its mark on the Windermere landscape to the present day. After the Norman Conquest, 'Forest Law' was imposed on much of the Lake District in order to preserve the game, and throughout medieval times large parts of Furness and the barony of Kendal were set aside for hunting. To the north, Inglewood Forest had become the largest hunting ground in England, while Copeland Forest and the royal hunting forest of Furness were barely of less extent. In each of these areas, forest laws firmly controlled the amount of wood which could be collected for domestic use, and 'assarting' – the clearance of the woodland for new farmsteads – was strictly prohibited. Prior to the foundation of Furness Abbey in 1127, the whole of High Furness had been under forest law, and the Coucher Book of Furness Abbey records that Stephen's grant to the abbot included 'all that my forest of Furness and Walney *with all privilege of hunting therein ...*'. The foundation of the abbey effectively removed the restrictions of forest law from the Furness Fells, and during the monastic rule much of the woodland was cleared and many new farms were established. But towards the end of the abbey's life, the pleasures of high living once again pervaded the monastic cloisters, and Abbot Banks launched a grand scheme to establish a large hunting ground on the abbey's estate. A site was chosen at Dale Park, covering the area between the Grizedale valley and the western shores of Windermere, and the existing tenants were ruthlessly ejected in c.1516 to make way for a deer park. Four centuries later it is a sobering thought to remember that this site is now one of the few places in Britain where native red deer can be found roaming wild amongst the woodlands.

To the east of Windermere the story is remarkably similar. Following the Norman Conquest, deer freely roamed the fells above Ambleside and Troutbeck, and hunting took place over a large proportion of the barony of Kendal. But as the population rose steadily during medieval times, more and more of the upland wastes were converted into sheep-runs and cattle pastures, and the deer were restricted to smaller and smaller areas, deliberately set aside for hunting. In 1225 William de Lancaster had been rebuked by Henry III for retaining too much of his lands in their natural state as hunting forest, and shortly after a small deer park was created in the upper Troutbeck valley, near The Tongue, the walls of which – enclosing the two-thousand-acre Troutbeck Park – can still be traced. At about the same time Sir Roger de Lancaster established a hunting reserve in the Rydal valley near Ambleside. In 1277 his neighbour, William de Lyndesey, was heavily fined for allowing his tenants' animals to stray into the precincts of the deer park. The wall which can clearly be seen today snaking its way up the spur of Scandale Fell above Ambleside village dates from this action, when William de Lyndesey promised to erect a fence to separate his sheep pastures in Scandale Bottom from the hunting grounds of Rydal Park.

Some evidence of the growing prosperity of the Windermere area at this time is preserved in the records of the Lay Subsidy of 1332, which was granted to King Edward III by Parliament in order to augment his royal revenues and to pay off the outstanding war expenses. This unpopular tax on the rich amounted to a fifteenth of each landowner's movable goods and chattels, and the tax assessment indicates that as many as eleven landowners were liable for payment in the township of Applethwaite, while twelve more taxpayers resided at Troutbeck or Ambleside.

During the twelfth century the manor of Windermere was still part of the parish of Kendal, an extensive parish established shortly after the creation of the see of Carlisle in 1122. Being at the centre of one of the largest parishes in England, Kendal parish church grew to almost cathedral proportions, financed by the wealth collected in tithes from the local woollen merchants. The fertile Windermere valley and the Vales of Grasmere and Rydal were steadily increasing in wealth and in population at this time, and the need for some further sub-division within the parish became more urgent to ease the burden of the long trek to Mass on the great saints' days, and the arduous journey to attend baptisms, weddings and funerals. By the beginning of the thirteenth century chapels-of-ease had been provided at

Bowness and Grasmere, but each of these daughter chapels lacked a graveyard, and mourners were still forced to accompany the corpse for many miles along the rough tracks to the mother church at Kendal.

The final blow to the system came in 1348, when the Black Death swept through the whole of the Lake District, claiming hundreds of victims in the Windermere area alone. No longer was it feasible to carry all the bodies to Kendal, and the order was given for the consecration of burial grounds at Bowness and Grasmere. The right to perform the sacraments precipitated the granting of parochial status, and St Martin's became the centre of the new parish of Windermere in 1348, while Grasmere followed shortly afterwards in 1349. Later chapels-of-ease at Troutbeck, Ambleside and Langdale subsequently became the centres of separate parishes, and the original parish of Kendal is now sub-divided into some nineteen smaller parishes.

A similar situation developed in the neighbouring parish of Cartmel. Prior to the dissolution of the monasteries, the whole of Cartmel Fell lay within the jurisdiction of Cartmel Priory. The charming little chapel of St Anthony's on Cartmel Fell – with its family box pews and three-decker pulpit – was founded originally as a chapel-of-ease by the Augustinian friars in 1504. On the dissolution of the priory in 1536, the priory lands fell into the possession of the Crown, and many of the buildings fell into ruin. But the parishioners were allowed to continue worshipping in the small chapel of St Michael, and in 1597 the parochial 'twenty-four' got to work repairing the priory church and restored it to its former glory for use as the parish church of Cartmel. St Anthony's Chapel continued to serve as a chapel-of-ease for the former tenants of the priory, and with the steady growth in population during the seventeenth and eighteenth centuries, it ultimately became a separate parish in its own right, being licensed for marriages in 1754, baptisms in 1764 and burials in 1765.

A constant and serious threat to the prosperity of the local inhabitants during medieval times came from north of the Solway. Throughout this period the Lake District was very much a disputed border region, and, although the English Crown remained the dominant force in the Windermere area after

William II's victory in 1092, the possibility of a raid by a band of marauding Scots was always very close. Although William II had established the border counties of Cumberland and Westmorland in 1120 as a bulwark against the Scots, on the death of Alexander I in 1124 his successor, David I, immediately claimed Cumbria as part of his rightful kingdom. In 1136 the Scots gained control of the Solway region as far south as the River Esk, and until 1154 – when the area was exchanged for parts of Northumberland – the northern part of Cumbria remained part of the Scottish kingdom of Strathclyde. Between the twelfth century and the fifteenth century, Scottish raids were frequent in the Lake Counties. Carlisle was besieged in 1173 and 1174, and again in 1215, though the thirteenth century was generally quite peaceful. A period of intense border conflict followed the crowning of Robert the Bruce as King of Scotland in 1307. Raids began in 1311, and in 1314 Edward II was defeated at Bannockburn. In 1322 Robert the Bruce plundered Holme Cultrum Abbey and marched south across the Duddon to Furness Abbey, where the abbot was forced to pay a princely ransom. The Scots continued their plunder at Cartmel Priory, crossed Morecambe Bay and burnt Lancaster to the ground before returning north through Westmorland.

In order to protect themselves from these northern invaders, many of the wealthier families of Southern Lakeland built themselves fortified manor houses or refuge towers where they could withstand a short siege, even if they lost some of their cattle and sheep. The fourteenth-century pele tower attached to the western end of Kentmere Hall is a splendid reminder of this period, as are the similar structures at Ubarrow Hall in neighbouring Long Sleddale, and at Wraysholme, near Cartmel. Each of these pele towers was built without windows on the ground floor, and the living-quarters were confined to the castellated upper storeys. The towers were accessible only by ladder from the outside and were designed to withstand a short siege by a group of Scottish raiders, who might, hopefully, move on to find easier plunder elsewhere.

The notable absence of pele towers in the Windermere valley itself has led some experts to suggest that the southern valleys of Lakeland were too poor to merit extensive raids by the Scots.

With pele towers occurring in neighbouring valleys, however, and with many tales of raiders coming down the Scots' Rake in the folklore of the Troutbeck valley, it seems more likely that the landowners of the Windermere valley resorted to other means of defence. Early in the fourteenth century the de Lindesays, for example, built their manor house on Long Holme (i.e. Belle Isle), a site well chosen for its easily defended position, while the de Lancasters obviously had the same end in view when they built Rydal Old Hall on the steep slopes overlooking the Rothay valley.

The Scottish raids remained a real threat to the livelihood of the local people throughout the fourteenth and fifteenth centuries, and whenever Scottish armies marched south, beacons were lit on Skiddaw, Hardknott and Coniston Old Man to warn of the invasion and to mobilize the contingents of local men on border service. Cumbrian men were amongst those who helped Edward III to defeat the Scots at Halidon Hill in 1333, while 'fellows fierce from Furness fells' fought bravely under the Earl of Surrey at Flodden. The English successes at Flodden Field in 1513 and at Solway Moss in 1542 effectively put an end to the large-scale border raids, but it was ultimately the accession of James VI of Scotland to the English throne, in 1603, which finally united the two kingdoms and ushered in a period of peace and prosperity on a scale hitherto unknown in the Windermere area.

7

Yeoman Farmers and Market Towns

The English countryside blossomed under the Tudors and the Stuarts. The victory of Henry Tudor at Bosworth Field not only marked the defeat of Richard of York but also established a dynasty which was to bring strong, effective government to the country and put an end to the vicissitudes of the Wars of the Roses. His son, Henry VIII, had not only been able to celebrate a crushing defeat of the Scots at Flodden but it was he – hungry for personal wealth – who confiscated thousands of acres of land from the monasteries and created a new class of landowner by selling the proceeds to the highest bidder. The glories of the first Elizabethan Age were evident throughout the realm, as the increasingly prosperous gentry rebuilt their homes in grand style, leaving a legacy of half-timbered Elizabethan mansions scattered around the countryside. And the accession of James Stuart, in 1603, finally brought an end to the constant border warfare which had sapped the strength of the northern marches for centuries, and created the political stability which was an essential prerequisite for a prosperous agriculture in the Lake counties. Even the climate of the seventeenth century aided the quietly growing wealth of the English countryside. Under the Tudors and the Stuarts, the climate of Britain was generally cooler but drier than at present – a factor which, no doubt, assisted agriculture and favoured the fortunes of the landed classes of Southern Lakeland.

The dissolution of Furness Abbey in 1537, and the growing prosperity of Tudor England, saw a rise in the prestige of the landed gentry of the Windermere area. To match their new status and wealth, the Tudor aristocracy built themselves new residences as an outward display of their affluence and local power. The Philipsons were the most powerful family in the parish of Windermere, owning several estates on the eastern shores and a fortified manor house on Long Holme. In 1566 they built Calgarth Hall, a beautiful Elizabethan mansion, whilst another branch of the family occupied Rayrigg Hall until the Flemings took over the estate in 1735. It was a member of the Philipson family, Christopher Philipson, who in 1629 composed the inscription visible today on the underside of an arch in St Martin's Church, to mark the failure of the Gunpowder Plot of 1605. The Philipsons also owned Hodge Hill in the parish of Cartmel Fell, while their neighbours here included the Knype family of Burblethwaite Hall and the Thorphinstys of Thorphinsty Hall. On the western shore the Sandys family established themselves as the leading family in the Hawkshead area, following the demise of Furness Abbey. Graythwaite Hall is an imposing mansion built by the Sandys family during Elizabethan times, while Esthwaite Hall was the seat of another branch of the family. Graythwaite Old Hall, on the other hand, is an earlier building, belonging to the Sawreys in the days of Henry VIII, and later becoming the home of the Rawlinsons.

The Civil War of the 1640s had little effect on the Windermere area, which, in common with most of northern England, was strongly Royalist. The unsuccessful siege of the manor house on Long Holme, by a party of Roundheads from Kendal, confirmed the excellent defensive site of the Philipson's stronghold, and only the organ in St Martin's Church, which was 'cutt in pieces', succumbed to the hostility of the Presbyterian opposition. The Protestant Reformation did, however, result in the loss – in all but name – of a prominent local landmark. In 1256 Walter de Lyndesay, Lord of the Manor, had established a small chapel, dedicated to the Virgin Mary, on one of the small islands of Windermere. St Mary's Chapel was a chantry chapel, served by two priests, where prayers for the dead – and especially for its founder – were regularly said. Generally the chantry had its own priests, but in the fifteenth century William de Biggynges is recorded as being not only 'parson of the Church of Wynandermer' but also chaplain of the chantry on

'Marieholme'. The original endowment of the chantry chapel included land on the neighbouring eastern shore of Windermere, and in 1352 this legacy included an estate at Fallbarrow known as 'Monkbarrow' or 'Frerefield'. In 1553 the remaining chantries were suppressed by Edward VI, and St Marieholme, together with the neighbouring land at Calgarth, Green Farm and Fallbarrow, was sold to Thomas Sidney of Wolsingham and Nicholas Halswell of Goudhurst. The chapel quickly fell into disrepair, and all that remains today is a flight of steps cut into the rock on the north side of the island, and the name 'Lady Holme'.

The Reformation brought a similar fate upon the ancient chapel dedicated to St Catherine, which stood beside the old trackway from Kendal to Ambleside where the road descends steeply to the valley floor near Troutbeck Bridge. By 1777, when Nicholson and Burn compiled their *History of Westmorland*, all that remained of the way-side shrine at St Catherine's Brow was distant memories. Today the chapel is all but forgotten, except for the names of the local mansions at St Catherine's and Chapel Ridding.

A more important result of the Reformation was the growing strength of Nonconformist denominations during the seventeenth century. Immediately following the Civil War, the Episcopal Church was disestablished, and in 1653 toleration was granted to all Christian sects except 'Papists' and 'Prelatists'. During the Commonwealth period which followed, Nonconformist preachers were free to roam across the country and to share their religious zeal with any who cared to listen. Foremost amongst these Dissenters was George Fox, founder of the Religious Society of Friends, who preached at Cartmel and Staveley during his first visit to the area in 1652. Quakers soon began to meet together in each other's homes, and in 1658 the Friends at Colthouse, near Hawkshead, purchased a small plot of land at Benson Orchard to be used as a burial ground for the members of their society. The small, white roughcast building, blending in with the other cottages, was built as a meeting house by the Friends in 1688.

The age of religious freedom, however, was short-lived, and following the Restoration of Charles II the Anglican Church was re-established and the Cavalier Parliament quickly passed a number of laws – known as the Clarendon Code – aimed at Nonconformist Dissenters. Renewed persecution of Nonconformists followed the Conventicle Act of 1664, which forbade religious meetings of more than four persons unless conducted according to the Book of Common Prayer. Fines accompanied a first offence, while imprisonment and transportation could result from subsequent convictions. George Fox himself sought refuge at Swarthmoor Hall, near Ulverston, where he was protected from persecution by Judge Fell. In 1678 a number of local men, including Isaac Dixon of Heaning, George Williamson of Bannerrigg and Richard Crewdson of Crook, were fined for attending a Quaker meeting in Bowness. The Windermere Friends, who met regularly at John Braithwaite's house at Mislet, were fined again in 1684 for non-attendance at the local parish church. In the same year a number of Quakers were fined for attending a meeting at the 'Mansion house of George Braithwaite' at High Wray, including 'William Satterthwaite, mercer, of Colthouse, Edward Satterthwaite, tanner, of Town End, Miles Birkett, yeoman, of Cartmel Fell, and Thomas Rawlinson, gentleman, of Graythwaite Old Hall'. The religious fervour of the meeting clearly appealed to all classes.

The Conventicle Act was followed the next year by the Five Mile Act, which prevented any Nonconformist minister from living or teaching within five miles of a borough. This act caused great hardship amongst Nonconformist preachers and led to the construction of isolated chapels in remote locations. The meeting house at Height – on the road between High Newton and Cartmel Fell – was erected here by the Friends in 1677, while the little chapel at Tottlebank, near Colton, was built by the Baptist brethren from Ulverston in 1669. Sometimes, as at Mislet, the Dissenters continued to meet in a private house, while on other occasions it was hoped that the purchase of a cottage to be used as a meeting place might rouse less suspicion than the construction of a new building. The Baptist chapel at Hawkshead Hill, dating from c.1678, was converted in this way from an old cottage. The chapel – re-opened for worship in 1977 – still retains its own small burial ground, and the old open-air baptistry can still be seen at the foot of the chapel garden. The Friends' Meeting House at Rook How, where the Satterthwaite and Dale Park roads meet, was erected in 1725 and was, in a similar manner, built as half cottage and half meeting house. These isolated Nonconformist chapels are a reminder of an age of religious intolerance, and only with the accession of William III, following the 'Glorious Revolution' of 1689, did the persecution of Nonconformists in this area come to an end.

Undoubtedly the greatest effect of the Protestant Reformation of the Windermere landscape was the dissolution of the monasteries by that greatest of all predators, Henry VIII. The confiscation of the abbey lands during the 1530s, and the redistribution of thousands of acres of agricultural holdings, created in England a new class of landowner – the yeoman farmer. Neither peasant nor lord, the yeoman represented a new breed of independent landowner, the new middle class, who worked their own land and did so much to improve the standard of English farming and the prosperity of the nation during Tudor times. With the dissolution of Furness Abbey in 1537, and the demise of Cartmel Priory in 1536, much of the area of High Furness and Cartmel Fell came into the hands of this new landed class. But even before Henry VIII passed the death sentence on the religious houses, the abbeys' tenants had already begun to wrest land, illegally, from the monasteries.

In High Furness small tracts of arable land had already been enclosed by some of the tenants of Furness Abbey by the end of the fifteenth century. These patches of land were enclosed piecemeal to keep out the abbey's sheep and to provide subsistence crops for the tenants' own consumption. As the prosperity of its tenants was in the abbey's own interest at a time when all the tithes went directly to the coffers of the abbot, the abbey found it expedient to come to some agreement on the matter. Accordingly in 1509 twenty-two tenants met at Colton and signed an agreement with the abbey whereby.

Every vjs viijd yerlie rente, which payeth iiijd for boundery shall have one acre and halfe of such ground as haith been of common pasture within tyme of man's mynde; and those tenantes that haith more then iiijd for vjs viiijd of yerelie rent to have there improvements more largelie, and those that payeth less then iiijd to have their improvements thereafter.

This agreement, and a later one signed in 1532 by forty-five tenants at Hawkshead Hall, allowed the enclosure of small areas of land, no larger than $1\frac{1}{2}$ acres, together with the building of a farmhouse. Such smallholdings were referred to locally as 'grounds' and often bore the name of the new owner. Many of the farms in High Furness still bear the name of the original tenants, and Roger Ground, Waterson Ground, Sawrey Ground and Thompson Ground are just a few of the farmsteads in the Hawkshead area which were established at this time. Over thirty grounds can still be identified in High Furness, though some of the names have subsequently disappeared from the map, especially when later buildings were erected on the same spot. Betty Fold, near Hawkshead Hill, for example, was built in 1907 on the site of Dodgson Ground, while nearby Borwick Lodge was formerly known as Borwick Ground. On the eastern shores of Windermere similar piecemeal enclosures were being claimed by the tenants of Cartmel Priory, and Simpson Ground and Bellman Ground date from this period. By the time Matson Ground and Low Millerground were established in the seventeenth century, the word 'ground' had taken on a wider meaning, referring to any small enclosure from the common land, but within the area of High Furness and Cartmel Fell the broad distribution of grounds shows that a major stage in the colonization of Southern Lakeland had already been reached *before* the dissolution of the monasteries.

From the dissolution in 1537 to 1662, the 'liberty and Lordship of Furness', including the manor of Hawkshead, lay in the hands of the Crown. The same fate overtook the parish of Cartmel from 1536 to 1640. It was during this period that the descendants of the monastic tenants and the new breed of smallholders succeeded in establishing their rights to the land on which their ancestors had farmed for centuries. In an agreement reached with Queen Elizabeth I in 1586, the emerging yeoman farmers gained the right to hand on their estate at death to their next of kin, so obtaining a security of tenure which was essential if they were to spend much time and effort in improving the quality of their holdings. This agreement, however, was made at a price. In the years preceding the unification of England and Scotland, all border tenures were negotiated with one eye on the mosstroopers and cattle-raiders from across the Solway, and each of the northern customary tenants was required to contribute towards the defence of the realm should the Scots move south. Notwithstanding this obligation to military service, the small holdings were now legally and firmly established in the hands of the new 'statesmen' farmers, and this new landed class had the incentive to improve and develop their land for their own financial gain.

In High Furness the agreement of 1586 consolidated the gains made by the tenants of Furness Abbey before the dissolution. In this area many of the yeoman farmers had already established their independence before the Crown took possession of the manor in 1537, but the agreement recognized the expansion of these small farmsteads into viable units and secured the tenure of other local yeoman farmers such as the Bensons of Skelwith Fold and the Taylors of Finsthwaite. To the east of Windermere the ranks of the rising yeoman class were swelled by the former tenants of Cartmel Priory, such as the Birkheads of Birket Houses, who took advantage of the priory's demise by enclosing parts of the common by dry-stone walls. Many of the farmsteads on Cartmel Fell date from this period, and over the next hundred years or so many of the farmhouses were rebuilt in stone, including Gill Head, Rosthwaite, Ludderburn and Hartbarrow. By the end of the eighteenth century the farmstead at Sow How was already being referred to as an 'ancient enclosure', and it is clear that other encroachments had been made on the commons during the seventeenth century. The legal position of these enclosed farmsteads was confirmed in 1640, when Charles I granted the former Priory lands of Cartmel to seven local landowners, 'in order that they may convey by deed to the rest of the tenants (hitherto holding of the Crown) their respective tenements'.

In the Ambleside area a Rental of 1675 records that by this date there were as many as forty-three yeoman farmers in the locality, each holding his land by customary tenure and handing on estates from father to son with a security of tenure unknown to earlier generations. In the township of Troutbeck no less than fourteen yeoman's houses were built alongside the road from Town Head to Town End during the seventeenth century. These included Low Fold, built in 1674, and Town Head, erected in 1693, while the 'Mortal Man' inn, constructed during Victorian times, was built around an old cottage bearing the date 1690. The 'Queen's Head', where for centuries the local shepherds have met before mustering the sheep from the common hill pastures, is a genuine seventeenth-century building, dating from 1631, though the former spinning gallery beside the Kirkstone road has been converted into a modern restaurant.

At Town End – a yeoman's house built by George Browne on his marriage in 1623 – the National Trust has restored the building and has re-created the atmosphere of a typical seventeenth-century statesman's home by furnishing the house with contemporary fittings, purchased from the Browne family in 1947. Town End displays the distinctive round chimneys typical of many of the seventeenth-century yeoman's houses, and in common with its neighbours it is tucked into the hillside and surrounded by trees to shelter it from the main blast of the wind. To keep out the draughts, the walls of the house were covered with a layer of roughcast, which was repeatedly coated with layers of whitewash. Only the walls of the barn were left bare, exposing the dull slabs of local slate directly to the elements. The barn at Town End is a large, two-storey building, built on the opposite side of the road to the house, providing a clear testimony to the wealth of its owners. The lower storey, accessible from the field below the barn, housed the byre, while above the heads of the cattle the upper storey consisted of a hay loft, accessible only from the road adjacent to the upper side.

Not all the yeomen were able to build on such a grand scale as at Town End, and many of the humbler statesmen's farmsteads consisted of a single building – a longhouse, comprising a farmhouse, a byre and a barn, all under one roof. The dwelling house was, again, the only part of the building to be covered with roughcast and whitewash, whilst the byre – built end-on to the house – was accessible, even in the worst weather, by an internal cross-passageway. Other unusual features of the vernacular architecture are found on many of the seventeenth-century yeoman's houses in the Troutbeck area. The original round chimneys are invariably set on top of a slate water-tabling, to protect the joint between the chimney stack and the roofing material, while the ridge often consists of heavy interlocking slates known locally as 'wrestler slates'. The gable ends are sometimes strengthened by heavy overlapping slates, forming 'corbie-stepped gables', while a low porch usually shields the front door from the worst of the weather.

The fact that the yeoman farmers of the Windermere area could afford to rebuild their houses and barns in *stone* during the seventeenth century is a reflection of the growing wealth realized from agriculture during Tudor and Stuart times. While the statesmen followed the lead of the monasteries and continued the profitable business of rearing sheep on the common upland pastures, they also concentrated more on the production of arable crops in the lower and more fertile fields. William Camden, riding through Westmorland in 1607, observed that there was plenty of arable land on the valley floors, while Celia Fiennes, passing through Windermere in 1695 on her *Journey through England on a side saddle*, noted that the commonest cereal grown was oats, eaten in the form of porridge or as a thin oatcake or 'clap bread'. As it was too wet for wheat, bigg (a species of barley) was grown for bread and for brewing, while peas and beans provided a staple diet, and potatoes were gradually introduced towards the end of the seventeenth century.

Since feudal and monastic times, arable farming on the lower land had been a co-operative venture, and parts of the valley floor were covered by open fields, worked in strips. The common land was usually divided into the in-field and the out-field, with most of the crops being raised on the heavily manured in-field. The out-field was generally left fallow, and hay was grown for use as winter fodder, though once every nine or ten years the out-field might also be planted with bigg or oats. At Hawkshead the old common field extended from the village centre south to Esthwaite Lodge, while the hamlet of Outgate probably grew up at the place where the enclosed fields of the valley floor joined onto the unenclosed common 'fell' land. At Ambleside the exact site of 'the old field' is unknown, but we do know that the out-field – where hay was grown – was enclosed, in spring, from the open common land of the in-field, by a temporary fence or 'floak'. This arrangement continued right up to the nineteenth century, and Wordsworth, in his *Guide to the Lakes*, published in 1822, noted that 'the arable and meadow land of the valley is possessed in common field; the several portions being marked out by stones, bushes, or trees.'

Oats and barley grown in the common fields were ground at the communal corn mill, which usually served the whole parish or township. The first record of a corn mill at Ambleside occurs in an inventory of 1324, prepared on the death of Ingelram de Gynes, husband of the heiress Christian de Lindsey and Lord of the Manor of Windermere. The original mill was situated on Stock Beck, occupying, perhaps, the same site as the seventeenth-century corn mill erected by the Braithwaites on the north bank below Stock Bridge. This later mill is still intact, though the present overshot wheel is a modern replica, and the premises have been converted into a shop.

In the township of Undermillbeck – the area surrounding Bowness – the first corn mill was in existence by such an early date that it gave its name not only to the stream on which it stood but subsequently to the township itself. The 'Mulnebec' is mentioned as early as 1220 in the Cartulary of Cockersand Abbey, so the mill itself must have been in existence by the beginning of the thirteenth century. Another mill, serving the township of Troutbeck, began its life before 1390 as a fulling mill. By 1649 the mill – at Troutbeck Bridge – had been converted into a corn mill, though in 1673 it was again converted, this time into a paper mill. Other local mills included the corn mill at Burblethwaite Hall, serving Cartmel Fell, Gilpin Mill near Crook, and the seventeenth-century mill at Skelwith Force, serving the township of Monk Coniston and Skelwith, while villagers from Hawkshead used the ancient manorial corn mill at Hawkshead Hall.

While oats, beans and barley were restricted to patches of land on the valley floors, the greater part of the valley sides and the upland commons were set aside for grazing. The increasing wealth of the Tudor yeoman farmers was based on their livestock – cattle, sheep, horses and occasionally a few pigs and poultry –

and this is reflected in the inventories of the period. When Thomas Williamson, a yeoman, of Common, in the township of Applethwaite, died in 1735, the main items recorded in his Will were:

Husbandry Gear and a Garner	£ 2.10.0.
Live Stock Beasts and a Horse	£16. 5.0.
Sheep Young and Old	£12. 0.0.
Pultery etc.	2/-6
Stocks of Hay and Straw, Bigg and Oats	£ 7. 0.0.
Meal, Malt and Household Provisions	£ 1.10.0.

Of all a yeoman's possessions, his sheep and cattle were the most precious, as these were the basis of his present prosperity and his security for the future. The wealth of a yeoman was determined largely by the number of sheep that he owned, but a farmer was not allowed to turn more sheep onto the open fells in the summer than he could winter on his own land. This led to some prosperous farmers renting or owning land and sheep in neighbouring parishes. When George Dixon of Heaning died in 1704, in addition to his own flock at Applethwaite he owned 120 'heave-going sheep' let to him to farm at Fell Foot in Little Langdale.

These 'heave-' or 'heaf-going' sheep were permanently kept on the same 'heaf' or pasture on the open fell and were either hired from the landlord or bought from the previous tenant and sold to the next incoming tenant on leaving the farm. As a yeoman farmer would wish to carry the maximum head of sheep on his holding, the land was carefully managed and apportioned to different uses at different times of the year. On the valley floor near to the farmstead, the 'inby' land – the most fertile land, covered perhaps by alluvial deposits – would be heavily manured and used for intensive winter grazing, if not already utilized for fodder crops or cereals. On the lower valley sides, 'intake' land would be enclosed from the common land by dry-stone walling, and the grass would be improved by cutting artificial drainage channels or by liming the soil.

Many of the dry-stone walls criss-crossing the undulating plateau of Claife Heights date from this time, as the yeoman farmers of Hawkshead reclaimed new pastures at Waterson Intake, Rough Hows Intake and Moss Eccles Intake, to name but a few of the enclosures. In the Troutbeck valley the head wall – separating the improved pasture of the intake land from the rough pasture of the open fell – runs as high as 650 feet on the west side of the valley, while, due to aspect, 475 feet is the more normal altitude on the eastern side. The rough, unimproved 'fell' land, above the intakes, was held in common, to be utilized for summer grazing. The farmers operated a system of transhumance or *saeterbruk*, whereby all the sheep and cattle were moved to the common pastures in the spring and were mustered again in the autumn to be allocated to the different farms, before being brought down to the inby land for the winter.

The sheep and cattle were turned out through the 'yeats' or gates which led via drove roads or 'rakes' to the common pastures on the higher fellsides. The gates or barriers which kept the livestock out on the fell were maintained at common expense, and at Ambleside a document of 1630, issued by the court baron of the manor of Windermere, warned of a fine if the tenants did not fulfil their obligations:

> It. That the High fell Yeats that are painable, Vizt. Scandale Yeat, the Steal Yeat and the Wall Yeat are to be made by the Tenants above Stock, and the Kirkstone Yeat and Water garth Yeat by the Tenants of beneath Stock, and whosoever shall not make and Hing them before the 24th Day of Apprill particularly Every year forfeits 6s 8d.

A similar fine could be expected if any yeoman failed to move his livestock up to the common pastures during the summer: 'Itm. It is ordered thatt noe Tenant in Ambleside shall suffer their Kine or Chattell to bee or remaine amongst their Houses or Doors beneath their Fineable yeats from Mid May till Michaelmas by the space of one day at one time upon paine of 6s 8d.'

At Troutbeck the common pastures or 'hundreds' were divided into three areas – the Upper, Middle and Lower Hundreds – while the township was similarly divided into three sections, and grazing rights were distributed accordingly. The Hundreds were reached by drove roads including Nanny Lane and the Hundreds Road leading up the fellside from the cattle gates in the vicinity of Longmire Yeat. Although, in time, these drift ways came to be walled in, this was not always the case, and in 1717 the court of the manor of Windermere fined a Troutbeck farmer 3s. 4d for driving his cattle 'from his ancient out Rake' through the Middle and Lowest Hundreds to Skelgill Close 'to the great disturbance' of his neighbours.

The yeoman farmers of the seventeenth century were largely self-sufficient, and the optimum use to which they put every available resource was an agricultural economy in the true sense of the word. As well as providing a source of bread, barley was grown for the production of home-brewed ale, and malt is a frequent item in the inventories of the period. Woollen fleeces from the sheep continued to be spun into yarn – often in the spinning galleries attached to the yeomen's houses – before being collected by the 'chapman' for despatch to the local weaver. In addition to hay, the leaves of the ash tree were carefully harvested as winter fodder for the cattle, but in the autumn any livestock which were surplus to requirements were slaughtered and salted down for winter provisions. The hides were tanned locally, and the leather used for saddles, bridles and belts. Near Longmire Yeat, in the Troutbeck valley, lie a field called 'Tanner's Close' and another nearby known as 'Pit Paddock', where there are still remains of a tanning pit. When George Williamson farmed Bannerrigg at the end of the seventeenth century, the small-holding included 'tann-yards', and Williamson was described as a 'tanner'.

Peat was the fuel used in the open fireplaces of the yeomen's houses, and this too was obtained locally. Every tenant had strictly defined rights to peat-cutting, and the *Orders for Troutbeck and Ambleside*, dated 30th November 1630, warn: 'Whosoe breakes any Garth or Hedge or takes any Peates in other Men's Mosse forfeits for every Default 6s 8d.'

During the seventeenth century tenants from Ambleside shared rights for peat-cutting on Stock Moss Common, while in 1764 plans were drawn up for three new common peat mosses at Snarker Moss, Bakestones Moss and Scandale Bottom, to be divided between the tenants from the Markett Stead quarter, the Lowest quarter, the How Head quarter and the Nook End quarter.

Any excess grain, wool or sheep could be sold at one of the new markets which sprang up in the Windermere area during the seventeenth century. At Ambleside a Royal Charter for a weekly market and a biannual fair was secured by the Countess of Pembroke in 1650. The weekly market, held in the market square on the site of the present market hall, took place on Wednesdays and was a purely local affair. The main items of trade were farm produce and wool, and, in a somewhat modified form, the market continues today, though the wool market was closed in 1825 when mechanization of the textile industry led to the collapse of the Kendal woollen trade. The Ambleside Fair, on the other hand, was a much grander spectacle. The fair provided an opportunity for a full-scale livestock market, and the streets of the town were filled with cattle for several days. Pedlars and clothiers arrived from different parts of the country, and the stalls were stacked high with sweetmeats, comfits and other edible luxuries, while acrobats, jugglers and ballad-mongers contributed to the general festivity of the occasion.

Before the founding of the market in 1650, the development of Ambleside had been confined to the hilly area above Stock Bridge. The earliest chapel, situated at the top of Chapel Hill, was already in existence in 1597 when the townsfolk decided to contribute towards the maintenance of a curate, to preach and to teach the children. Prior to 1674, Ambleside above Stock was part of the parish of Grasmere, while Ambleside below Stock was part of the parish of Troutbeck. But that year the residents of Ambleside petitioned the bishop of Chester for the right to perform baptisms, marriages and burials, and Ambleside became a parish in its own right. The old chapel continued to double up as the local school until 1725, when the Free Grammar School was built nearby under the bequest of John Kelsick, a local merchant.

The area adjacent to Chapel Hill, Peggy Hill and Smithy Brow formed the ancient nucleus of the early settlement. Just below the old chapel lies How Head – a grand example of a seventeenth-century yeoman's house, complete with its round chimney and slate inter-tabling, whitewashed walls and wrestler slates surmounting the ridge. The area between Smithy Brow and Stock Ghyll was known as Braithwaite Fold and was occupied by the house and mill belonging to the Braithwaites – the leading family of Ambleside during the seventeenth and eighteenth centuries. The Braithwaites were of yeoman stock, holding their Ambleside estate by customary northern tenure, though subsequently they bought land in Langdale, at Brathay, and beside Pull Beck. The family gained their wealth by selling wool, barley and leather, and the inventory made on the death of Gawen Braithwaite in 1653 included 357 sheep at the Rigge, 200 sheep at Baisbrowne in Langdale and at Pull Beck, various cattle, horses and oxen, and 5 barns containing 80 stones of wool, 114 bushels of barley malt, 80 bushels of barley and 80 bushels of oats.

The vast quantities of malt were required for the brewing house which the Braithwaites operated at Braithwaite Fold, while the oats and barley were ground at the Braithwaites' own mill on the north bank of 'Rattle Gill', below Stock Bridge. Just below the corn mill, water from the headrace was carried across Stock Beck in a wooden trough to the seventeenth-century bark mill, situated on the opposite bank. This mill, which remains largely intact, crushed the bark in order to extract tannin, which was then used to cure leather at the Fisherbeck Tannery, south of the village.

The home of the Braithwaites was a modest house facing onto Smithy Brow. The house contained thirteen rooms, with outhouses including the brewhouse. The stockyard, surrounded by hay barns and byres, probably opened onto North Road, while a small garden led down to the beck. The stream itself was bridged by the attractive Bridge House, built in 1723 as a summer house and apple store, and leading to the Shaw Wife Orchard beyond Stock Beck. The Bridge House is now owned by the National Trust and stands beside the main road to Rydal, built across the garden of Braithwaite Fold in 1833.

The Braithwaites, in common with other yeoman families, grew in wealth and influence because of successful farming and careful management. They also lived in an age where raging inflation favoured their pockets, as, while prices increased fivefold during the sixteenth century, the customary rents remained fixed. As a result, the value of the customary rents decreased, and from late Tudor times onwards many of the yeomen were able to buy the freehold on their own property. Some yeoman families completed the climb up the social ladder to gentility and became accepted members of the landed gentry. During the reign of Elizabeth I the Braithwaites purchased the manors of Baisbrowne, Burneside and Warcop, and the family became armigerous in 1591.

As the Braithwaites rose in importance, the modest family home above Stock Beck became known as Ambleside Hall, while Ambleside expanded under their influence, away from the old core on Chapel Hill, down towards the new market-place below Stock. The rising industries of Tudor times and the increasing level of trade created a new class of townspeople who had no property of their own and had no claim to the common land of the township. These labourers or cottagers were provided with small houses by their employer, and at Ambleside the Braithwaites built cottages below Stock Beck for their growing workforce of artisan labourers. None of these new tenements possessed the right to take peat from the common peat mosses, so the Braithwaites arranged for their workers to cut peat at Brathay, where they owned suitable moss-land.

As Ambleside expanded on the land below Stock, several ale-houses grew up to serve the needs of the new wage-earning artisan class. By 1691 there were six ale-houses in Ambleside, including the 'Black Cock' – the earliest inn in Ambleside, which stood on the site of the Queen's Hotel – and the 'Salutation', which opened for business in 1656.

Whatever their importance, the Braithwaites were far from being the only employers in Ambleside during the seventeenth century. By late Tudor times the township had a number of mills, most of which were located on the 'Old Mill Lands' surrounding Rattle Gill. As well as the Braithwaites' corn mill and the bark mill, the waters of Stock Beck also turned the wheel of a sawmill – later converted into a woollen mill – near the Braithwaites' summer house. Further upstream, the site of Horrax's nineteenth-century bobbin mill was occupied by an old corn mill operated by the Jackson family in 1639, while immediately upstream stood a medieval fulling mill – one of three fifteenth-century fulling mills recorded alongside Stock Beck in a Rental of 1494.

In addition to the woollen industry, Ambleside was also a centre of papermaking, and a document of 1681 records that Richard Compston purchased an oak tree from Sir Daniel Fleming of Rydal Hall 'for an Axletree for his Paper Mill'. Compston's paper mill was situated on Scandale Beck, some distance above Low Sweden Bridge, where the ground next to the stream is known as 'Paper-mill Coppice'. It was Richard Compston's son who converted the corn mill at Troutbeck Bridge into a paper mill in 1673, and the family are still remembered today by the street named after them in Edwardian times. Another local street name commemorates John Kelsick, the seventeenth-century grocer who founded the grammar school, while other contemporary Ambleside craftsmen included William Benson, the draper, and Lancelot Benson, a saddler.

To the west of Windermere, the seventeenth-century also saw the growth of Hawkshead from a small village into a thriving market town. During the reign of Furness Abbey, Hawkshead had always remained subservient to the abbey's market town at Dalton, in whose parish it lay. Following the dissolution, the townsfolk petitioned for the right to perform baptisms, weddings and funerals, and Hawkshead became a separate parish in 1578. The church was substantially enlarged during the sixteenth century by Edwin Sandys, Archbishop of York, who had been born in Hawkshead in 1516. The grammar school, also founded by Edwin Sandys, followed in 1585, although the present building dates from 1675.

It was the Sandys family, in the person of Adam Sandys, who ensured the future prosperity of Hawkshead in 1608, by obtaining the charter for a weekly Monday market and a biannual fair. As at Ambleside, the market was largely a local matter, but the two annual fairs – at Easter and in October – attracted agricultural labourers from far afield and brought clothiers and pedlars from distant corners of the country. The fairs were a keenly awaited event in the lives of the local population. They provided the townsfolk with their only opportunity of buying in stocks of salt, spices and other 'luxuries' which the local market traders could not supply. The fairs were usually held on saints' days or other holy-days, when the parishioners would first attend church and then sample the delights of the fair. The fairs were carefully timed to fall at Easter – when depleted winter stocks could be replenished after the season of Lent – and in the autumn, when stocks could be laid in for winter.

During the seventeenth century Hawkshead became the chief market centre for the whole of High Furness, and the lucrative wool trade, conducted with merchants from Kendal, guaranteed the success of the new venture. For two centuries Hawkshead throve as a busy regional market town, and ultimately the collapse of the market in the nineteenth century was largely due to the demise of the Kendal woollen industry. In its heyday, Hawkshead market presented a busy, bustling scene of activity. The stalls erected in the market square were piled high with eggs, poultry, leatherwork and hand-woven cloth, while on the south side the market hall was occupied by the 'shambles', where butchers from various parts of the parish came to trade in mutton and beef. Beyond the market-place, the narrow passageways and archways connecting Hawkshead's three main squares and numerous yards would be thronged with people, while the 'Red Lion' and the 'Crown and Mitre' provided hospitable welcome for the local yeoman farmers.

Not all the villages and towns in the Windermere area had such scenes of thriving prosperity during the seventeenth century. Although the markets at Ambleside and Hawkshead were both a resounding success, another attempt to create a market town – at Staveley, in Westmorland – ended in dismal failure. Staveley was granted a market charter as early as 1329, but this valiant attempt to create a thriving town failed because of the close proximity and overriding dominance of Kendal's market, founded in 1189. And although Windermere became a large and prosperous parish in 1348 – the year of the Black Death – longstanding attempts to develop the village of Bowness into a thriving market town met with only a very limited success.

Perhaps the reason for this lack of growth stemmed from the fact that Bowness itself lay almost directly on the ancient pack-horse route from Hawkshead market to Kendal. The route from Hawkshead skirted Esthwaite Water before passing over a marshy area near Sawrey where a causeway – formed from juniper and ling, covered with gravel – was constructed to improve the track. The pack-horse trains crossed Windermere at the site of the modern ferry and continued across Undermillbeck Common on their way to Kendal. In the years before 1750 a team of six pack-horses regularly made the journey from Hawkshead to Kendal twice a week, while another team of horses made regular trips from Hawkshead to Whitehaven, reaching Langdale via Rothay Bridge – an ancient pack-horse bridge which has since been widened. In 1635 the Windermere ferry sank with the loss of forty-seven lives, and the list of victims included 'wool-workers', 'shear-men' and other local craftsmen on their way to Kendal.

Another ferry route crossed Windermere some two miles to the north, where the bridlepath from Hawkshead across Claife Heights met the lake shore at Belle Grange. From here, the ferry crossed to Low Millerground, where the belfry on the gable end of the cottage, built in 1612, housed a bell which could be used by passengers to summon the ferry boat from Belle Grange. Local residents visiting this spot recall the legend of the 'Crier of Claife', whose voice, they say, can still be heard on stormy nights calling across the lake for a boat.

The waters of Windermere itself were also used for transport during the seventeenth century, when iron ore was carried up the lake from Low Furness to the bloomsmithy at Cunsey Beck. Although bloomeries for making iron had been banned temporarily by Queen Elizabeth's decree of 1565, by 1623 a bloomsmithy, or forge, had been established beside Cunsey Beck, half a mile upstream from Cunsey Bridge. A bloomsmithy consisted of both a bloomery hearth and a water-powered trip hammer, and at Cunsey a headrace carried water from a small millpond to the forge site on the south bank of the beck. Little remains at the site today, but a small farm building beside the track was once used as the office. Other local bloomsmithies included those at Force Forge in the Grizedale valley and at Low Wood near Haverthwaite, while at Backbarrow, in 1685, James Machell built a weir 210 feet across the River Leven to divert the water to power his bloomery forge.

Backbarrow was also the site of the first blast furnace to be constructed in the North of England, in 1711. The furnace was built by William Rawlinson and John Machell, and the first blast ran from the middle of June in 1712 to the end of February in 1713, producing 514 tons of iron. Throughout the eighteenth and nineteenth centuries the ironworks produced bar iron for chains and anchors, and cast-iron cooking-pots for export to West Africa and the West Indies. The village of Backbarrow expanded as rows of workers' cottages were erected alongside the forge shops and storage sheds. The Backbarrow ironworks ceased production as recently as 1965, and, although the furnace, dated 1711, is still intact, the storage sheds have rapidly fallen into decay.

In the same year as the Backbarrow blast furnace was built, Edward Hall of Cranage in Cheshire purchased the bloomsmithy at Cunsey and proceeded to build a rival blast furnace at Cunsey Bridge, on the site of the later bobbin mill. A weir by the bridge directed water along the headrace to power the forge hammer, while the blast for the furnace was obtained by a large pair of water-powered bellows.

All these early bloomsmithies and furnaces used charcoal to heat the ore, and, as the century progressed, supplies of suitable wood had to be fetched from further and further afield. Even in 1623 an agreement made between 'William Wrighte of Cunsey, in the parish of Hawkshead, Forgeman' and the Pennington family of Muncaster reveals that fuel for the bloomsmithy had to be brought all the way from Hacket Ground in Little Langdale. By 1663 there was such country-wide concern over the shortage of timber for the British Navy that a national census of trees was carried out, which recorded only 1,218 timber trees in the whole of the parish of Windermere. Although coppiced woodland was not included in the survey, the results revealed an alarming shortage of trees in the Windermere area. A more recent study, using pollen analysis of the peat bogs and lake sediments of High Furness, has confirmed that much of the area was virtually stripped of trees by the middle of the seventeenth century. The realization of the extent of this problem, and the subsequent re-afforestation of the Windermere fell-sides from the 1750s onwards, marked a distinct change in the attitude of the local landowners and opened up a completely new chapter in the development of the Windermere landscape.

8

The Romantic Age

By the middle of the eighteenth century, the valley sides and fells surrounding Windermere were clothed with fewer trees than at any other time since man first settled in the area. Centuries of grazing by numerous flocks of sheep, and the voracious appetite of the smelting industries, had resulted in the denudation of vast areas of fellside. Although there were extensive stands of oak trees at Brathay and Pull Woods, and several areas of coppiced woodland on the eastern shore and in the lower Troutbeck valley, the Windermere landscape was generally much more open and barren than it is today. The steep slopes of Claife Heights and Gummer's How were covered with rough grassland, gorse and bracken and were almost bare of trees, while the Grizedale valley was flanked by steep moorland pastures, utilized extensively as sheep-runs.

Towards the end of the century, coniferous trees first began to make a major contribution to the Windermere landscape. In 1783 the Browne family of Town End, Troutbeck, planted over a thousand seedlings, consisting mainly of Scots pine but including smaller stands of silver fir, white American spruce and some Balm of Gilead firs. In 1788 another six thousand Scots pines were planted, and subsequent afforestation included stands of larch, Egyptian poplar and Norway spruce. New species of deciduous trees, including sycamore and beech, were also introduced during the eighteenth century, and extensive plantations around Beech Hill date from this period. When Nathaniel Spencer journeyed beside Windermere in 1771, he observed: 'The south east shores are covered with wood, cut into distinct plantations, and running to the top of lofty mountains.' In 1784 over 20,000 trees were planted on the Pull Woods and

Brathay estate, including 9,500 Scots pines and 1,500 larches, as well as many spruce, ash, birch and willow.

One of the foremost of all the eighteenth-century planters was John Christian Curwen, whose wife Isabella purchased the house on Long Holme in 1781. It was the Curwens of Belle Isle who were responsible for the extensive afforestation of Claife Heights and to whom the present wooded landscape owes much of its character. In 1798 John Christian Curwen planted thirty-thousand larches on the steep slopes of Claife Heights, while the gentler slopes and more promising patches of land were seeded with acorns.

Another ardent agricultural improver was Richard Watson, Bishop of Llandaff, who resided at Calgarth Park from 1789 and was awarded a gold medal by the Board of Agriculture. During 1805 and the following year, Watson created an extensive plantation of 322,000 larches on the slopes of Birk Fell and Gummer's How, replacing the degraded sheep pastures with a growing commodity that could be marketed for pitch, tar, resin or turpentine, as well as for constructional purposes.

On the open moor at the head of Grizedale, Montague Ainsley of Grizedale Hall planted over $1\frac{1}{2}$ million larch trees during the nineteenth century. The Ainsleys were primarily industrialists who owned haematite mines and ironworks in the Dalton area, and the barren uplands of Hawkshead Moor were planted as much for aesthetic reasons as for financial gain.

Today the extensive plantations of larch and pine covering the slopes of Claife Heights and Gummer's How, and the mixed woodlands surrounding Graythwaite Hall and Pull Wyke, combine to make Windermere one of the most artificially landscaped of all the Lakeland valleys, and most of these plantations came into being around the end of the eighteenth century.

However obvious their presence today, the numerous stands of coniferous trees planted since 1780 should not eclipse the importance of the ancient coppiced woodlands of the Windermere area. During the eighteenth century extensive areas of birch, oak and hazel continued to be harvested every fourteen or fifteen years for the production of charcoal or for other traditional woodland industries. Throughout the nineteenth century birch and willow from Rayrigg Woods was used to make swill baskets – boat-shaped baskets woven from flat strips of wood. These 'swills' were used in coal mines or for potato-picking, while the shallower oak swills or 'spelks' were used for delivering bread. From Middleton's swill-making workshop at Mill Stile, near Spark Bridge, the swills were despatched for use by charcoal burners, by farmers and housewives and in bobbin mills.

As the Lancashire cotton industry expanded during the nineteenth century, the woodlands of the Windermere area became the centre of yet another new industry which sprang up to serve the needs of the flourishing textile trade. The invention of water-powered spinning frames, capable of spinning hundreds of threads at the same time, created the need for countless wooden bobbins to hold the finished yarn. This demand was met by the development of bobbin mills, where coppiced wood was cut into slices and bored through by a 'rincer', before being turned on a water-powered lathe.

The first bobbin mill in the Windermere area was opened at Skelwith Bridge in 1789 by Jeremiah Coward. The Skelwith Bridge bobbin mill – which operated until 1871, on the site of the present slate works – produced bobbins for the Lancashire cotton mills and also made boxes for the Elterwater Gunpowder Company. In 1829 the old mill at Troutbeck Bridge was converted into a bobbin mill, and it continued to turn bobbins until 1900, when it was converted once again – this time into an electricity generating station. Horrax's bobbin mill, beside Stock Ghyll above Ambleside, dates from 1839 and is still largely intact, though the machinery was sold in 1964 and one of the former coppice sheds has since been converted into holiday flats. At Thursgill Mill, by the deep ravine below Hawkshead Hill, a breast wheel once turned the lathes producing bobbins, spools, spindles and pulleys, while swills, barrels and hoops were also made at the mill.

Other local bobbin mills included the Staveley mill, employing over two hundred workers in 1860, and bobbin mills at Force Forge and at Cunsey Beck. At Stott Park, near Finsthwaite, the bobbin mill was first opened in 1841 and greatly extended in 1880. The mill continued in production right up to the 1970s and has since been restored by the Department of the Environment and opened to the public.

Much of the afforestation which took place in the Windermere area in the late eighteenth and early nineteenth centuries would have been impossible had not the open fellsides and moorlands been enclosed and brought into private ownership. Piecemeal enclosure of common land had been taking place since monastic times, and much of the improved pasture on the lower slopes consisted of 'intake' land which had been reclaimed from the common fell. But from the middle of the eighteenth century enclosure became much more systematic, and during the 1790s, when the war with France caused food prices to rise to an all-time high, the demand for increased agricultural production prompted a number of enclosure schemes.

In 1796 a private Act of Parliament was passed, 'for improving, dividing and enclosing the commons, waste grounds and mosses in the parish of Cartmel, in the county palatine of Lancaster'. The enclosure of the common pastures of Cartmel Fell brought a major change to the appearance of the landscape. Allotments of land were made to all those who held rights of pasture on the commons, and twenty-four public carriage roads were laid out to connect the new allotments to the existing settlements. Birket Houses was linked in this way to Birket Houses Allotment by a 'public carriage road, branching from High House Road, and bounded by allotments made to James Birkett Esq., and Mr. Joseph Latham, on the east, and by the land undisposed of and Mr. John Pool's allotment on the west, leading by Gill Head to Bowness.' The winding course of the present main road between Newby Bridge and Bowness, and passing close to Stewardson Nab, has its origins in 'Another public carriage road from Town Head, northwards over the commons by Birch Hill, and to an ancient lane and highway leading through John Stewardson's estate towards Bowness.'

These enclosure roads were well built, to a carefully specified standard:

The road to be regularly formed and covered with stones not less than 12 ft wide, and nine inches thick in the middle or crown of the road, and five inches at the hem or skirt, exclusive of a covering of

three inches thick in its whole breadth of good samel or small
gravelly substance, and the stones to be well broken and none of
them to exceed the size of a goose's egg.

In order to pay for the new roads and drains, and to meet the
costs of the Enclosure Commissioners, some of the common land
was sold by auction to the highest bidder. Successful buyers
included John Pool, who acquired 287 acres near Gill Head, and
Bishop Watson of Calgarth Park, who purchased 784 acres of
common near Gummer's How, which he subsequently planted
with larches in 1805.

In addition to the many public carriage roads, seventy-nine
private carriage roads and driftways were also constructed at this
time, including

> Another private carriage and driftway from the said Crosthwaite
> Road, of the breadth of 15 ft, westwards over allotments severally
> made to the Poor and School of Cartmell Fell, and John Rawlinson,
> to Foxfield, and from Foxfield northwards over allotments severally
> made to the said John Rawlinson and Susannah Dodson, into the
> said Crosthwaite Road again, near the Ashes, and which we call
> 'Foxfield Road'.

Many of these roads, such as Foxfield Road and High House
Road, are today little more than cart-tracks, bordered by the
dry-stone walls erected at the time of the enclosure awards,
though some of these enclosure roads – like the Newby Bridge
Road from High Newton to Canny Hill – still form the basis of
the routes followed by our main roads today.

The common lands of Claife Heights were enclosed by a
private Act of Parliament secured by John Christian Curwen in
1794, and, following the enclosure awards five years later, the
steeper slopes bordering Windermere were planted with
thousands of larches and oaks. The flatter land on the top of
Claife Heights was enclosed by dry-stone walling and converted
into productive pasture-land. John Curwen was a leading
agricultural reformer of his day and travelled extensively in
Britain and on the Continent to study new techniques of
farming. Following the lead of Charles Colling, Curwen was a
prominent breeder of Shorthorn cattle, and the fields which he

created on the plateau of Claife Heights were stocked with early examples of this new breed.

John Curwen was also a close friend of Arthur Young, the Secretary of the Board of Agriculture set up in 1793, and was very much influenced by the new ideas of the Agricultural Revolution. On his tour of the Lake District in 1770 Arthur Young had observed thousands of acres of 'waste land' in Cumberland and Westmorland and had suggested that much of it might be enclosed and reclaimed for pasture or arable land. The latest techniques of farming proposed by Arthur Young included the introduction of new crops such as turnips and clover and the five-year rotation recorded by Young himself in the Keswick area in 1768, where years of fallow and sown grass alternated with arable crops of wheat, barley and oats. Pasture was also improved at this time by liming the soils, and several lime-kilns were erected along the Coniston Limestone outcrop at Borwick Ground, Sunnyhow, Wray and Pull Beck, after Bishop Watson had encouraged the use of coppiced woodland for burning the lime.

Further enclosures of common land in the Windermere area followed at the beginning of the nineteenth century. An Act of Parliament of 1813 led to the enclosure of Undermillbeck Common and the allocation of 2,199 acres of agricultural land in 1822. Applethwaite Common and the Troutbeck Hundreds were also enclosed by separate Acts of Parliment, in 1831, though it was some eleven years before the land was allocated to the local yeoman farmers. By the time of the General Enclosure Act of 1845, the most promising agricultural areas of Southern Lakeland had already been enclosed by common consent or by private Act of Parliament, and very little Parliamentary Enclosure is recorded throughout Lancashire and Westmorland after 1845. In the Windermere area 1,161 acres of Scandale Fell was enclosed in 1845, but the growing opposition to the enclosure of the commons during the 1860s and 70s, and the success of the Commons Preservation Society in the country at large, prevented the remaining commons from being enclosed. Today the greater part of Loughrigg Fell and Rydal Fell remains as unenclosed rough pasture and open to the public for their enjoyment.

Hand in hand with the eighteenth-century enclosure of the commons came the decline of the small yeoman farmer. Wordsworth noted this change in the landscape and observed that the number of 'statesman' farmers had been halved between 1770 and 1820. This reduction in the number of freehold farmers was accompanied by a large increase in the average size of holdings, as smaller farms became amalgamated and the larger, more successful farmers bought out the freeholds of those who were struggling to make a living. The demise of the yeoman farmer resulted from a number of causes, of which the enclosure of the common pastures was only one contributory factor. Other reasons included the inability of the smallholders to compete with newer and more efficient agricultural techniques adopted by the larger landowners in the lowlands, while the movement of the traditional spinning and weaving activities away from the domestic spinning galleries to the textile mills of Lancashire and Yorkshire deprived the yeoman farmers of an additional source of income. Many of the 'statesmen' in the Windermere area were forced to sell their smallholdings and either move to the local towns or sink to the lower social position of agricultural labourers. This movement down from the ranks of the yeomen created an emerging class of 'cottagers' in the growing settlements of Ambleside, Staveley and Kendal.

At the opposite end of the social scale, the purchase of large tracts of freehold land in the latter half of the eighteenth century was accompanied by a great influx of new landowners into the area from amongst the ranks of the wealthy and educated upper classes. The building of large mansions on the shores of Windermere dates from this period, following the lead of Thomas English, a Nottingham merchant who in 1774 built the Round House on Belle Isle, to the design of John Plaw. This cylindrical mansion – the first round house to be built in Britain – was also the first house in the Windermere area to be situated and constructed entirely for aesthetic reasons. The building was carefully sited to command a magnificent view across Bowness Bay, and, with its Ionic columns and towering dome, the mansion was designed as a piece of art rather than as a practical refuge from the wind and the rain. The house and island were purchased in 1781 by Isabella Curwen of Workington Hall, shortly before her marriage to John Christian, and the landscaped gardens were laid out soon afterwards by Thomas White. John Christian – who added his wife's surname to his own after his marriage – also planted the many trees which today partly obscure the round house from view and help to conceal the limited width of the island.

The next large mansion to grace the Windermere landscape was Brathay Hall, built in 1788 by Mr Law of Old Brathay. High Brathay – as the new Georgian house was originally called – soon became the home of John Horden and subsequently passed into the hands of the Redmayne family in 1834. It was Giles Redmayne who, in 1836, built Holy Trinity Church, Brathay – a tiny Italianate structure, perched on top of a small drumlin and looking uncomfortably out of place below the rugged crags of Loughrigg Fell.

In 1789 Richard Watson built his fine Georgian mansion at Calgarth Park, with its landscaped lawns leading gracefully down to the eastern shores of Windermere. Bishop Watson was the son of a master of Heversham grammar school and subsequently went up to Cambridge and achieved a brilliant academic career. He became a Fellow of the Royal Society and was awarded the Chair of Chemistry, before later being appointed Professor of Divinity. His appointment as Bishop of Llandaff was largely a political affair, and Watson resided permanently at Windermere, visiting his diocese only once during his career. As a scholar and academic, he was typical of the new breed of landowner who dominated Windermere society by the middle of the nineteenth century.

Farther down the lake, Storrs Hall was built in 1790 for Sir John Legard, who in 1804 erected the octagonal garden house now known as 'Storrs Temple', at the end of a stone causeway built out into Windermere. 'The Temple of the Heroes' was erected in honour of Admirals Duncan, Howe, Vincent and Nelson and, in common with nearby Finsthwaite Tower, commemorates the British naval victories of the Napoleonic Wars. In 1806 Storrs Hall was acquired by John Bolton, a Liverpool shipping merchant, and by 1811 the architect Gandy had transformed the hall into a large and elegant Georgian mansion. Bolton lived at Storrs until his death in 1837, and more recently the Hall has been converted into an elegant hotel.

Storrs Hall was followed in 1808 by Elleray, a modest Georgian house near Orrest Head, built by John Wilson of Paisley, who, as 'Christopher North' of *Blackwood's Magazine*, managed to secure sufficient patronage to be elected Professor of Moral Philosophy at Edinburgh University. As the nineteenth century progressed, a lakeside mansion on the shores of Windermere became a fashionable proposition, and The Briery, built in 1850 for the great educationalist Sir James Kay-Shuttleworth, was followed by Huyton Hill and Langdale Chase in 1891, and by Blackwell – built by Baillie Scott for Sir Edward Holt – in 1900.

Of all the nineteenth-century mansions, perhaps the most unusual is Wray Castle, built in the style of a medieval fortress by Dr James Dawson, a retired Liverpool surgeon, in 1840-47. The castle is typical of some of the wilder fantasies indulged in by the early Victorians and looks notably incongruous on the gentle wooded slopes of Watbarrow Point.

Of the many famous nineteenth-century personalities who came to associate themselves with the landscape of Windermere, no doubt the most celebrated of them all was William Wordsworth. Wordsworth was born in 1770, the second son of John Wordsworth of Cockermouth, chief attorney to Sir James Lowther and steward of the manor and forest of Ennerdale. Williams' mother, Anne, died when he was only eight years old, and he was sent to lodge at Anne Tyson's cottage while he attended Hawkshead Grammar School from 1778 to 1783. In 1787 Wordsworth went up to St John's College, Cambridge, and ultimately settled at Dove Cottage, Grasmere, with his sister Dorothy in December 1799. Wordsworth remained at Grasmere until 1808, during which time he wrote many famous poems and the fourteen books of 'The Prelude'. A short period at Allan Bank was followed by the move to Rydal Mount in 1814, where Wordsworth remained in residence until his death in 1850. Throughout this period at Rydal, Wordsworth continued to publish a prodigious output of poems, sonnets and letters, and many of his verses not only reveal his love of the Lake District but also give us a moving insight into the romantic beauty of the Windermere landscape.

Of his school-days, Wordsworth wrote, in 'The Prelude':

When summer came,
Our pastime was, on bright half-holidays,
To sweep along the plain of Windermere
With rival oars; and the selected bourne
Was now an Island musical with birds
That sang and ceased not; now a Sister Isle
Beneath the oaks' umbrageous covert, sown
With lilies of the valley like a field;
And now a third small Island, where survived
In solitude the ruins of a shrine
Once to Our Lady dedicated and served
Daily with chaunted rites. In such a race
So ended, disappointment could be none,
Uneasiness, or pain, or jealousy:
We rested in the shade, all pleased alike,
Conquered and conqueror.

In the peaceful calm of 'An Evening Walk', Wordsworth evoked the tranquillity of the Lakeland vales:

Far from my dearest Friend, 'tis mine to rove
Through bare grey dell, high wood, and pastoral cove;
Where Derwent rests, and listens to the roar
That stuns the tremulous cliffs of high Lodore;
Where peace to Grasmere's lonely island leads,
To willowy hedge-rows, and to emerald meads;
Leads to her bridge, rude church, and cottaged grounds,
Her rocky sheepwalks, and her woodland bounds;
Where, undisturbed by winds, Winander sleeps;
'Mid clustering isles, and holly-sprinkled steeps;
Where twilight glens endear my Esthwaite's shore,
And memory of departed pleasures, more.

As a celebrated literary figure, Wordsworth drew around himself a sizeable following of poets and writers, some of whom visited the author at Dove Cottage or Rydal Mount and others of whom settled in the Windermere area. Samuel Taylor Coleridge was a frequent companion of the Wordsworths around the turn of the century, while de Quincey moved into Dove Cottage in 1809 after the Wordsworths departed. Sir Walter Scott first visited Dove Cottage in 1805 and proceeded to climb Helvellyn in the company of William Wordsworth and Sir Humphrey Davy.

Robert Southey, the Poet Laureate, who resided in Keswick from 1803 to 1843, was another frequent visitor, while from 1839 until his death in 1849 Hartley Coleridge, the elder son of Samuel Taylor Coleridge, lodged at Nab Cottage, near Rydal.

The literary intelligentsia of the day often met together at Brathay Hall, or at Old Brathay, and in 1825 a dinner party to celebrate Sir Walter Scott's fifty-fourth birthday was given by the Boltons of Storrs Hall and attended by Wordsworth, Southey, John Wilson and George Canning. A regatta the following day, organized by Professor Wilson, led to the initiation of a regular Sports Day, held annually by the old Ferry Inn until 1861, when the sports were transferred to Grasmere. The Ferry Sports of 1857 included a performance by Thomas Longmire, the Troutbeck wrestler, and a graphic account of the proceedings was published in Charles Dickens's *Household Words*.

Shortly before Wordsworth's death in 1850, Harriet Martineau, the celebrated writer and sociologist, came to live at The Knoll, on Rydal Road, Ambleside. Between 1847 and 1876 she was responsible for bringing many leading statesmen and literary figures to the shores of Windermere, and during this period several notable people came to reside in the Ambleside area. Harriet Martineau's visitors included not only Gladstone, Disraeli and the Prince of Wales but also famous writers such as Charles Dickens, Charlotte Brontë, George Eliot and Waldo Emerson. The educated élite of the late nineteenth century came to see Ambleside as an intellectual haven, and many Victorian mansions were built on the rocky slopes overlooking the Rothay valley. Eller How, on the road to High Sweden Bridge, was the home of Anne Jemima Clough, the first principal of Newnham College, Cambridge, from 1852 to 1862. In 1833 Dr Arnold, the celebrated headmaster of Rugby, built Fox How on the slopes below Loughrigg Fell and used it as his holiday home from 1836 to 1842. Nearby, Fox Ghyll was the home of W.E. Forster, instigator of the 1870 Education Act and Irish Secretary from 1880 to 1882.

The popularity of the Lake District amongst the wealthier classes of society during the nineteenth century has many root causes but stems not least from the glowing accounts of the district which began to appear in the popular magazines and journals of the day. Before the end of the eighteenth century the mountainous region of north-west England had been considered to be an area of unattractive moorland and a cultural desert, while the genteel, sophisticated members of society had preferred to sample the delights of Paris, Vienna and Milan on their 'Grand Tours' of Europe. The outbreak of the war with France in 1793 put an end to the 'Grand Tour', and prompted the 'idle rich' to seek new horizons for their amusement.

The first article to extol the virtues of the Windermere landscape appeared in the *Gentleman's Magazine* in 1748. This was followed by the accounts of numerous travellers who ventured beyond the frontiers of contemporary civilization to marvel at the raging torrents and the rugged crags of the Lake District. Gray's *Journal*, describing his journey through the region in 1769, and Gilpin's *Observations*, of 1772, stirred the emotions of a privileged élite who were eager to participate in this increasingly fashionable 'wilderness experience'. By the time West's *Guide to The Lakes in Cumberland, Westmorland and Lancashire* was published in 1778, it had become the accepted practice for wealthy visitors to travel from 'station' to 'station', savouring the extensive panoramas afforded from a number of pre-selected viewpoints which had been carefully chosen by previous travellers.

Having informed the reader in his *Introduction* that the Lakeland tour would 'furnish prospects no less surprising ... than the Alps themselves', West proceeded to outline his itinerary and to describe the view obtained from his selected 'stations'. Windermere itself could best be observed from five of these stations, starting at the foot of Claife Heights above the 'horse-ferry on Windermere-water' and proceeding via Belle Isle to Rawlinson's Nab, and on to Rayrigg Bank, where the prospect 'if not the most superlative view that nature can exhibit ... is more fertile in beauties than the reach of my imagination will allow me to conceive'. The view across the lake from West's First Station, on the slope above Ferry House, provided a visitor with the best introduction to the Windermere landscape:

The rock rises perpendicularly from the lake, and forms a pretty bay.

In front, Ramps-holme, or Berkshire-island, presents itself in all its length, cloathed in wood. To the left, the ferry point, closing with Crow-holme, a wooded island, forms a fine promontory. Just behind this, the mountain retiring inward, makes a semicircular bay, surrounded with a few acres of the most elegant verdure, sloping upward from the water's edge, graced with a cottage in the finest point of view. Above it, the mountain rises in an agreeable wildness, variegated with scattered trees, and silver-grey rocks.

To the north the vista opened up beyond the shrub-covered slopes of Claife Heights, whilst, directing one's gaze further to the right,

The eastern view is a noble contrast to this, adorned with all that is beautiful, grand, and sublime. The immediate space is much cultivated. The variety of hanging grounds are immense, consisting of woods, groves, and inclosures, all terminating in rocky uplands of various forms. It spreads out above in a beautiful variety of waving inclosures, intermixed with hanging woods, and scrubby circular spots, over-topped with wild grounds, and rocky ridges of broken mountains. In some places it swells into spacious bays, fringed with trees, whose bushy heads wave beautifully over the crystal waters. The *parsonage house* is seen sweetly seated under a range of tall firs. Following the line of shore, above the last ferry point, and on the banks of the bay, the tops of the houses, and the church of Windermere are just seen. Above that *Bannerig* and *Orrest-head* rise gradually into points, cultivated to the top, and cut into inclosures. These are contrasted by the rugged crags of *Biscot-how*. Troutbeck-park comes next in view, and over that, Hill-bell rears his comic top, and Fairfield swells in Alpine pride, rivalled only by Rydal's loftier head.

The romantic pictures painted by the writers of the early guidebooks are rivalled only by the equally exaggerated panoramas depicted by the early landscape painters. Artists such as Joseph Farrington, in the 1770s, distorted the perspective of the hills and valleys to such a degree that, on canvas at least, they really *did* seem to rival the precipitous slopes of the highest Alpine peaks. This over-dramatization of the landscape was not, however, the only technique used by the early visitors to improve upon the impression gained by the naked eye. West, for example, recommended that 'To render the tour more agreeable, the company should be provided with a telescope for viewing the fronts and summits of inaccessible rocks.' And if the exaggerated, larger-than-life effect was not to the visitor's liking, West had another suggestion: 'The *landscape mirror* will also furnish much amusement, in this tour. Where the objects are great and near, it removed them to a due distance, and shews them in the soft colours of nature, and in the most regular perspective the eye can perceive, or science demonstrate.'

The landscape mirror, or 'Claude Glass', consisted of a convex mirror, 4 or $4\frac{1}{2}$ inches in diameter. The visitor would turn his back on the scenery and would proceed to view the landscape within the restricted framework of the convex mirror. To get the best picture, West recommended *two* glasses of different convexity – a dark glass for use in sunshine, and a silver foil for use on more cloudy and gloomy days.

The Claude Glass was quickly followed by a further invention – the Gilpin Glass. This consisted of a set of glasses with different-coloured tints – a convenient device for the visitor who might otherwise be unable to visualize how the landscape would appear in spring, summer, autumn and winter. As a logical extension of this idea, the summer-house erected by the Curwens at West's First Station included a bay window glazed with a series of differently coloured panes. Not all the contemporary writers were enthusiastic about the psychedelic effect, but few would have disagreed with West when he concluded of Windermere: 'It will, however, perhaps be allowed by all, that the greatest variety of fine landscape is found at this lake.'

The most illustrious of the many guidebooks following in the steps of Thomas West's was undoubtedly Wordsworth's guide, published originally as the *Introduction* to Wilkinson's *Select Views in Cumberland, Westmorland and Lancashire*, in 1810, and issued as a separate volume in its own right in 1822. By the time the fifth edition was published in 1835, Wordsworth's *Guide to the Lakes* had become a best-seller.

Wordsworth was passionately in love with the Windermere landscape and recommended that, 'One bright unruffled evening must, if possible, be set apart for the splendour, the stillness, and solemnity of a three hours' voyage upon the higher division of the

Lake.' Wordsworth's *Guide* was written in romantic vein, and it is no surprise to find that he sadly lamented the lack of ruined castles and other ancient remains. Of Lady Holme he wrote: 'Every one must regret that scarcely a vestige is left of the Oratory, consecrated to the Virgin, which stood upon Chapel-Holm in Windermere.'

It was no doubt this love of ancient tradition, and Wordsworth's belief in the unchanging immortality of the landscape, which prompted a hostile response from him to the large-scale introduction of conifers in the late eighteenth century. Wordsworth complained: 'Other trees have been introduced within these last fifty years, such as beeches, larches, limes, &c., and plantations of firs, seldom with advantage, and often with great injury to the appearance of the country.' Yet when tradition clashed with Wordsworth's romanticized view of the landscape, it was the romantic vision which took precedence. Following the contemporary advice of Sir Joshua Reynolds, Wordsworth believed that local dwellings ought to blend in with the colour of the soil, and in his guide he criticized the traditional whitewashed cottages at length, declaring a marked preference for the 'cases where the glare of whitewash has been subdued by time and enriched by weather-stains'.

The romantic feelings of Wordsworth's day live on into the twentieth century in the Victorian place-names which replaced some of the older names in the Windermere area. Until 1853 the small bay to the north of Calgarth Park was traditionally known as 'Craam's Bay'. In that year two young men drowned nearby during a storm, and a small white cross was erected as a simple memorial. Conscious of the clear moral inscribed on the stone – 'Watch therefore for ye know neither the day nor the hour', the Victorians re-named the spot 'White Cross Bay', which it remains to this day. An earlier gesture of remembrance came in 1840, when Queen Adelaide, the Dowager Queen of King William IV, visited Windermere and stepped ashore at Low Millerground. The Queen ascended Rayrigg Bank to view the scenery, and, in honour of the occasion, the hill was re-named 'Queen Adelaide's Hill', while the 'White Lion' inn at Bowness, where the Queen dined, adopted the proud title of 'The Royal Hotel'.

Storrs Temple, built in 1804 to commemorate the heroes of the Napoleonic Wars

Wray Castle, a Victorian mansion built for Dr James Dawson

A corner of old Hawkshead, near the parish church

Wordsworth Street, Hawkshead

The Old Grammar School, Hawkshead, where Wordsworth studied as a boy

The Windermere Ferry and the well-wooded slopes of Claife Heights

The Windermere Hotel, built at the terminus of the Kendal and Windermere Railway in 1847

Belsfield, formerly the home of Furness industrialist H. W. Schneider

Moss Eccles Tarn, Claife Heights—a favourite spot of Beatrix Potter

St Martin's, Bowness, the parish church of Windermere;
rebuilt after a fire in 1480

The new launch *Miss Cumbria* moored at Shepherd's, Bowness

Sailing-boats moored near Ferry Nab

The *Swan* off Belle Isle

Old fishermen's huts and Sepulchre Hill, Bowness

The early romantic guidebooks, epitomized by the writings of West and Wordsworth, were superseded in time by descriptive guides which were more objective and which did not demand of the reader such a willing suspension of disbelief. By the middle of the nineteenth century guides such as Murray's *Handbook to the Lakes*, published in 1867, were beginning to cater for a clientele rather different from the aristocratic *voyageurs* of the late Georgian era. This change in readership led to the publication of M.J.B. Baddeley's classic guide for fell-walkers in 1886 and ultimately created the popular demand for a detailed walkers' guide to the fells – a demand admirably met since the 1950s by Wainwright's superb series of pocket guides. This change in emphasis, from guides for the stately 'viewer' to those catering for the active 'doer', reflected the growing divergence in the tourist market – a trend which coincided with improvements in transport, enabling the less wealthy classes to join in the enjoyment of the Lake District landscape.

9

The Coming of the Railways

When the first popular account of the Windermere landscape appeared in the *Gentleman's Magazine* in 1748, there was not a single well-surfaced carriage-road in the district. The stony track leading from Hawkshead to Kendal was passable only by pack-horse traffic, and the drove roads which led from the fellsides down to the valley floors were more suited to the slow-moving cattle than to the horse-drawn carts which would move an occasional load of hay, or which might sometimes be called upon to carry a coffin for burial at the nearest parish church.

The first local turnpike trust was founded in 1761, to improve and maintain the quality of the road between Kendal, Ambleside and Keswick. When Thomas Gray made his famous journey through the Lake District in 1769, he commented on the excellence of the new road which he followed along the shores of Thirlmere and on to Kendal. The trust was largely involved in improving the surface of the existing tracks, though here and there a new section of road was brought into being. At Ambleside the earlier pack-horse route leading to the north left the village via Chapel Hill and Low Sweden Bridge before skirting the lower slopes of Rydal Fell on its way to Grasmere. The newly established turnpike preferred the lower route across Stock Bridge and then down Smithy Brow to join what is now the main road following the shores of Rydal Water and Grasmere. The 'short cut' past the Bridge House and across the lawns of Ambleside Hall was only adopted in 1833. A second turnpike road was established near the foot of the lake in 1763, when the Kendal to Dalton road was turnpiked across Cartmel Fell and through the Backbarrow Gorge. Once again, the new carriage-road was far superior to the old pack-horse track, though not as straight as the 'New Causeway' laid in 1816 and followed by the present main road across Levens Moss.

The well-surfaced carriageways developed by the turnpike trusts were such an improvement on the old trackways which preceded them that William Wilberforce – who spent several summers at Rayrigg Hall – remarked in 1788 that, 'the banks of the Thames are scarcely more public than those of Windermere.' The improved carriageways led to a remarkable growth in traffic, both of goods and of passengers. With the advent of roads built to handle heavy wheeled traffic, pack-horses were soon superseded by the slow but reliable carriers' waggons. These heavy wooden carts were drawn by four strong 'bellhorses', each carrying bells hung around the neck to warn other travellers of their approach, for the cumbersome waggon teams were given precedence over lighter and more manoeuvrable vehicles.

In contrast, well-to-do passengers were propelled at the amazing speed of twelve miles per hour by the four-in-hand pulling the brightly painted stage-coaches. By early Victorian times Rigg's mail coaches ran a regular service from Windermere to Ambleside and over Dunmail Raise to Keswick, while in the summer the *Jenny Lind* completed a daily passage across the ferry and on through Hawkshead to Coniston. The development of coaching traffic led to the growth of coaching inns such as the 'Salutation' in Ambleside, and the 'Red Lion' in Hawkshead, where the horses could be changed in the inn yard while the passengers downed a cheering drink and grabbed a bite to eat in the friendly warmth of the cosy hostelry. The growth of regular stage-carriage services also brought about the change from a hand-rowed ferry to a steam-operated craft across Windermere in 1870. The resulting increase in traffic led to the building of the new Ferry Hotel in 1879, replacing the earlier Ferry Inn and occupied today by the laboratories of the Freshwater Biological Association.

Travel by stage-coach, however, was still relatively expensive and was limited to the financial resources of the upper and middle classes. Even in 1884 the fare from Windermere to Keswick was 7 shillings – an amount equivalent to almost a week's pay for many Manchester Victorian mill-workers. A somewhat cheaper method of travel was introduced in 1819 with the opening of the Lancaster Canal to Kendal. Moderately wealthy visitors could travel from Preston to Kendal in a 'flyboat' – a light passenger craft, pulled by two horses at a canter and infinitely more comfortable than the bumpy ride of a stage-coach.

The era of really cheap travel had to wait, however, for the opening of the Windermere Railway in 1847. Proposals for the building of a branch line, from the Lancaster and Carlisle Railway at Oxenholme to the lake shore at Low Wood, near Ambleside, were first put forward by Cornelius Nicholson, the owner of the paper mill at Burneside, near Kendal, in 1844. The proposals were immediately attacked by William Wordsworth, who wrote a strong letter of protest to the *Morning Post* alleging that 'artisans and labourers' and other such 'uneducated persons' would be quite incapable of appreciating the beauties of the natural scenery:

Go to a pantomime, a farce, or a puppet-show, if you want noisy pleasure – the crowd of spectators who partake your enjoyment will, by their presence and acclamations, enhance it; But may those who have given proof that they prefer other gratifications continue to be safe from the molestations of cheap trains pouring out their hundreds at a time along the margin of Windermere.

Owing to engineering difficulties necessitating a £12,000 viaduct across the Troutbeck valley, and a great deal of opposition from landowners such as the Earl of Bradford, whose estate at St Catherine's lay along the route of the proposed railway, the course of the line beyond Orrest Head was abandoned, and a new terminus was proposed about a mile away from the lake, near the hamlet of Birthwaite. With this compromise, many of the landowners were satisfied, but Wordsworth, enraged by their acquiescence and still utterly convinced that 'the imperfectly educated classes are not likely to draw much good from rare visits to the lakes' sent his famous sonnet to the *Morning Post*:

Is then no nook of English ground secure
From rash assault? Schemes of retirement sown
In youth, and 'mid the busy world kept pure
As when their earliest flowers of hope were blown

Must perish; – how can they this blight endure?
And must he too the ruthless change bemoan
Who scorns a false utilitarian lure
'Mid his paternal fields at random thrown?
Baffle the threat, bright Scene, from Orrest-head
Given to the pausing traveller's rapturous glance:
Plead for thy peace, thou beautiful romance
Of nature; and, if human hearts be dead,
Speak, passing winds; ye torrents, with your strong
And constant voice, protest against the wrong.

Despite Wordsworth's impassioned plea, work on the Kendal and Windermere Railway commenced in July 1845. The main line from Lancaster to Oxenholme, together with the branch line as far as Kendal, was opened to traffic in September 1846, and on Tuesday 20th April 1847 the line was opened throughout its length to the new Windermere Station, near Birthwaite. Wordsworth's worst fears – that the railway might yet be extended along the shores of Windermere – quickly assumed the air of distinct possibility when, at the opening luncheon held at the Royal Hotel, Bowness, Cornelius Nicholson addressed the assembled dignitaries with an enthusiastic proposal:

> We propose to enable the merchant princes of Liverpool, and the cotton-lords of Manchester, to exchange in a few hours the smoke of their factories, and the miasmata of their towns, for the salubrious airs and silvery mists that float round the hills you are now among. The railway will be extended along the shoulders of yonder hill, like a Swiss gallery, carrying it along past the remains of that old King of Cumberland who sleeps on the summit of Dunmail Raise, disturbing his remains, and perhaps scattering his ashes, till we meet other lines which will then give the Lake District the full benefits of railway communication.

Despite the construction of a cutting along St Catherine's Walk, the railway was never extended beyond Birthwaite, though further attempts in 1875 and 1887 to take the line on to Keswick and Ambleside promoted active, and successful, opposition from John Ruskin and Canon Rawnsley and led to the setting-up of the Lake District Defence Association, an early conservation society formed to protect the area from inappropriate developments.

The Windermere Railway soon gained a brisk traffic in both freight and passengers. Goods wagons arriving at Windermere brought in an assortment of fish, fruit and fresh vegetables for the local shops, coal and salt for domestic use, and saltpetre from Germany for the gunpowder works at Elterwater. The goods were unloaded into the railway warehouse or despatched immediately by horse and cart to the waiting customers. On their return journey the trucks were loaded with horses and cattle, timber, stone or coarse gunpowder from Elterwater, destined for the coal-mines of Lancashire or the slate quarries of North Wales. The main revenue, however, came from passenger trains. Regular services connected with the main line at Oxenholme, and from 1849 special excursion trains came from as far afield as Manchester, Leeds, Liverpool and Glasgow. The advent of cheap workmen's tickets made the Windermere area accessible, for the first time, to the artisan classes of Lancashire, and as a result the area immediately around Windermere Station became a hive of activity and the bustling centre of a thriving new settlement.

To the north of the station, Rigg's Windermere Hotel was opened by Richard Rigg in 1847 – the same year as the railway. Rigg's yellow-and-black coaches provided a connecting service from Windermere Station to various parts of the Lake District. To the south of the station, the cottages in Cross Street were erected during the 1850s, and Windermere village began to expand down Victoria Street and Crescent Road in the direction of Bowness and the lake. When Harriet Martineau wrote her *Complete Guide to the English Lakes* in 1855, she began, 'Now there is a Windermere railway station, and a Windermere post office and hotel – a thriving village of Windermere and a populous locality. This implies that a great many people come to the spot; and the spot is so changed by their coming and by other circumstances that a new guide book is wanted.' Windermere did, indeed, change very rapidly, and by the 1880s there were over forty lodging-houses in the village, in addition to many substantial villas, a school, several shops, a fire station and two churches – St Mary's on Ambleside Road, built originally in 1848 by the Reverend J.A. Addison who lived nearby in a substantial mansion known as Birthwaite Abbey, and St John the Evangelist, on Lake Road, consecrated in 1886.

The Kendal Railway was not, however, the only branch line to discharge visitors on the shores of Windermere. In 1850 the Furness Railway Company completed its line from Barrow and Dalton to Greenodd, and in 1868 the route was further extended along the Backbarrow Gorge to a new terminus at the foot of Windermere. The new line immediately attracted goods traffic from the local gunpowder works at Low Wood, and products which had previously been shipped by barge down the River Leven to Greenodd were now carried on a narrow-gauge tramway across an iron-girder bridge to Haverthwaite Station. The bridge across the Leven still remains, though the track has long since gone. Other traffic included 'Dolly Blue' from the ultramarine works at South Mill, Backbarrow, and coal, timber and beer – which were transported to houses and hotels alongside the lake by the Furness Railway Company's cargo vessel, the *Raven*.

The prime reason for the extension of the line, however, was the growing potential of a flourishing tourist traffic. The new Lakeside branch terminated at a large rail-and-boat interchange modestly described as 'a miniature Parkeston Quay', where three long platforms were constructed for the expected boom in traffic, and a restaurant and refreshment pavilion were provided for the convenience of day-trippers. From this impressive lakeside station, the visitor could cruise along the entire length of the lake, stopping off at Bowness for lunch and sailing on to Waterhead in time for afternoon tea. The coming of the railways was accompanied by the launching of the first steamers on Windermere, the paddle-steamer *Lady of the Lake* being commissioned in 1845, followed by the *Lord of the Isles*, the *Dragonfly* and the *Firefly*. The opening of the Lakeside branch was followed by the launching of the Furness Railway Company's first screw-steamer, the *Swan*, which heralded a new era in the size and comfort of the vessels navigating Windermere. The *Swan*, later replaced by another vessel of the same name, was followed in 1891 by the *Tern*, now the oldest of the 'Sealink' fleet operating on the lake. Each of the present boats was built at Barrow, subsequently dismantled and carried by rail to Lakeside and then reassembled and fitted out.

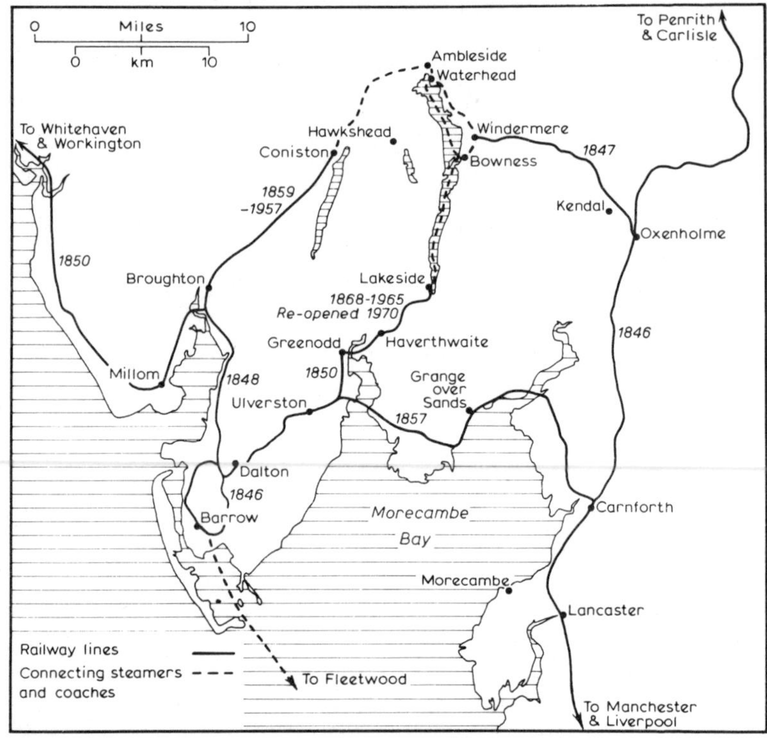

The railway network in the Windermere area

From the 1870s onwards, excursion trains from the mill towns
of Lancashire became a common sight at Windermere, and a
leisurely sail along the length of the lake might be followed by a
stroll to Ambleside, before the return trip to Lakeside. By the
end of the century, the itinerary for a day trip from Blackpool
could include a sail across Morecambe Bay from Fleetwood to
Barrow, the journey by rail to Lakeside and then a cruise along
Windermere. This might be followed by tea at Ambleside, before
continuing the journey by coach to Coniston, from where the
train returned to Barrow in order to catch the steamer back to
Fleetwood. Cowper, writing in 1899 in a less than enthusiastic
tone, blamed the 'cheap-trip system' for 'slowly but surely

ruining, sentimentally, the Windermere district':

> A crowded train arrives at Lakeside, and the steamer, packed with trippers so densely that they can hardly stir, whirls them away to the discordant sounds of the concertina, past the Ferry Hotel, to Bowness or Ambleside, where they are landed and regaled by brass bands and nigger troupes; and where, perhaps, meeting the tide of another cheap trip, brought by the London and North Western Company to Windermere Station, they continue to turn this unfortunate district into a perfect pandemonium.

During the Victorian era, private sailing-vessels were a luxury confined to the wealthier middle and upper classes, and elegant steam launches such as the *Dolly*, built in 1850, and the *Otto*, launched in 1896, were a regular sight on the lake. Due to the enthusiastic work of G.H. Pattinson and a team of willing volunteers, several of these stately launches can be seen today cruising up and down the lake, or as part of the permanent display at the Windermere Steamboat Museum, opened in 1977. Some of these vessels were owned by the wealthy families who came to reside by the shores of Windermere after the opening of the Kendal and Windermere Railway, and at Langdale Chase, for instance, the owners had a splendid boathouse specially built for their elegant steam launch, the *Lily* (since renamed the *Branksome*). During the 1870s Charles Fields of Sawrey operated the traction engine *Lavinia*, which he used to haul timber in the plantations behind the Sawrey Hotel. In the summer he would dismantle the engine and install it inside the *Fairy Queen*, a small paddle-steamer used for his enjoyment. By the end of the century, electric launches were navigating the waters of Windermere, and in 1899 the bobbin mill at Cunsey Bridge was converted into an 'Electric Works' at which the batteries of the electric launches could be recharged.

Another vessel which, for many years, operated regularly on the lake was the steam yacht *Esperance*, built for the Furness industrialist H.W. Schneider when he came to reside at Belsfield overlooking Bowness Bay, in 1869. Schneider owned iron mines in Low Furness and was a Director of the Furness Railway Company, and, following the opening of the Lakeside branch in 1868, he travelled daily from his home in Bowness to his work at

Barrow-in-Furness. As Schneider walked down the garden path to the Esperance Pier each morning, he was invariably preceded by his butler, carrying breakfast on a silver tray. Having enjoyed a leisurely meal on the journey to Lakeside, Schneider then boarded a special train which conveyed him swiftly to his office in Barrow.

Of all the influential people who came to reside on the shores of Windermere during the nineteenth century, Schneider probably had more direct influence on the growth of the settlement pattern than had anyone else. The expansion of Bowness from the 1870s onwards was, to a large extent, engineered by the speculative building programme launched by Schneider. Before the coming of the railways, Bowness had remained a small, tightly knit community, huddled among the narrow streets near Windermere parish church. The oldest cottages – including Laurel Cottage, which housed the first village school – were situated around Ash Street and Lowside, where the New Hall Inn – one of the oldest remaining buildings – dates from 1612. In Parson and White's *History, Directory and Gazeteer of Cumberland and Westmorland*, published in 1829, Bowness is described as

> ... a small but neat *market town*, in Undermilbeck township ... It is the chief port on the lake, and has a few fishing vessels, a number of pleasure boats, and a trade in charcoal and slate ... From its admirable situation it is much frequented by tourists, and has excellent accommodation for them in two good inns, the *White Lion* and the *Crown*, as well as in lodgings.

A small market was held every Wednesday, but the October Fair had already become obsolete.

During the 1830s and 40s, a number of private mansions, such as Belsfield and Ferney Green were built away from the original village centre, and a new grammar school was erected by Colonel Bolton of Storrs Hall, in 1836. But Bowness only started to expand *rapidly* after the opening of the Kendal Railway in 1847. This was followed by an influx of holiday-makers, and the Old England Hotel was opened in 1859 to cater for this expanding trade.

The one-inch Ordnance Survey map of 1865 shows the first signs of housing development along Elim Grove and beside Helm Road, and by the 1870s Bowness was already growing outwards along Lake Road towards Windermere Station. The shops along Crag Brow – including Frank Robinson's Fent Shop – were beginning to set up business at this time, while further along the road wealthy visitors were encouraged to take the waters at the Old Bath House, still standing beside the main road in the grounds of Thornburrow House. This trade in remedial bathing reached its peak in 1881 when the Windermere Hydropathic Hotel, situated on a rocky knoll overlooking the village, was opened to the public.

At this point Schneider began to build rows of elegant terraced villas to the north-east of the village centre, and much of the property found today in the Craig Walk district, between Lake Road and Biskey Howe, dates from this period. Schneider was also the chairman of the Bowness Board of Guardians and was responsible for the building of the almshouses on North and South Terrace. As Bowness grew in size and importance, the prosperous inhabitants took it upon themselves to renovate St Martin's Church, rebuilt and reconsecrated in 1483 after an earlier building had been destroyed by fire. A full-scale Victorian 'restoration' was carried out in 1870, completely changing the shape of the tower, incorporating a new chancel and obliterating much of the earlier interior decoration. The east window of the church, however, still retains a great deal of fifteenth-century stained glass, which was probably rescued from Cartmel Priory on its dissolution in 1536. Other early decorations still visible today include eight sixteenth-century inscriptions on the spandrels between the arches in the nave, and the arms of several prominent northern families, including the Washington family – ancestors of George Washington, first President of the United States. Outside the church, some of the ancient yews in the churchyard were probably planted at the rebuilding of the church in 1483, while others are estimated to be as much as seven hundred years old.

Bowness was not the only lake-side settlement to expand during the nineteenth century due to the growth of the tourist trade. As soon as the Windermere Steam Yacht Company set up their terminus at Waterhead in 1845, the village of Ambleside began to expand rapidly and to grow outwards towards the lake. Elegant mansions such as Rothay Holme (1854) and Loughrigg Brow (1863) were built to the south-west of the village centre, while more compact villas were constructed alongside Lake Road, leading to the steamer pier.

As Ambleside grew, the old parish church on Chapel Hill (now St Anne's Hall) was no longer sufficient for the needs of the expanding population, and the new parish church of St Mary was built in Gothic style by Sir George Gilbert Scott between 1850 and 1854. The transfer of the church from Above to Below Stock marked a new phase in the southwards growth of Ambleside, and the church was followed shortly afterwards by the removal of the old grammar school to the new school buildings on Vicarage Road.

The town hall and Mechanics' Institute, situated in the market-place, were built in 1858, while the market hall itself was rebuilt in Victorian Gothic splendour in 1863, and the market cross was moved to its present site on the corner of North Road to facilitate the flow of traffic. During the 1880s new building programmes progressed along Church Street and Rothay Road, while Compston Road – running in a straight line from St Mary's Church to Rydal Road – was cut in 1906. Meanwhile, during the 1890s the old mill lands were covered by a prosperous new Victorian suburb called Millans Park, and the Methodist chapel was built in elegant Tudor style in 1898.

The Ambleside chapel is one of several Methodist chapels that mark the phenomenal growth of Methodism in the Windermere area during the nineteenth century. John Wesley himself made at least nine visits to Ambleside, and these are all faithfully recorded in his *Journal*. Of his first visit, in April 1751, he remarked, 'the next day we rode to Ambleside, and On Saturday, 13, over more than Welsh mountains to Whitehaven.' In an age of spiritual hunger and pastoral neglect, Wesley's powerful preaching appealed to the hearts of many in the lower and lower-middle classes. The early converts met in their own homes and established a system of 'class meetings' for prayer and Bible study. Encouraged in spiritual growth by their own class leaders and by visiting 'local preachers', these meetings soon formed the nucleus of growing Methodist societies. The Methodist chapels at Bowness and Windermere both date from the period of rapid urban development following the opening of the Kendal and Windermere Railway in 1847. The tiny chapel at Hawkshead, however, has a quite different origin, dating from 1862 when Mrs Satterthwaite – a member of the Society of Friends at Colthouse – bought four cottages in one of the small squares and converted one of these into a small Free Church chapel. The building was formerly known as the 'Union Chapel', as all Nonconformist denominations were invited to worship here. Subsequently it was handed over to the Methodist Church after the death of its founder.

Since the end of the nineteenth century there has been relatively little new housing or commercial development in the centre of the major settlements, and Ambleside, Bowness and Windermere still retain much of their flamboyant Victorian character, reflecting the prosperity that was showered upon them by the forerunner of the twentieth-century tourist industry.

10

The Twentieth Century

The development of the Windermere landscape during the twentieth century is to a large extent a reflection of the growing influence of the tourist industry on the lake and its surroundings. During the nineteenth century the ownership of small, private boats was confined to the upper classes, and early yachts were sailed by fishermen from Morecambe Bay on behalf of the wealthy owners. Sailing, however, gradually became the pastime of a much wider cross-section of the public. In 1860 the first of the yachting associations – the Windermere Sailing Club – was founded, and in the 1880s the members rented a clubroom at the Old England Hotel. The club organized regular regattas on the lake, which attracted large crowds of wealthy visitors, and in 1887 the club received a royal warrant and became known as the 'Royal Windermere Yacht Club'. Over the years the membership has expanded to include the owners of many small yachts and dinghies, and today the club boasts an elegant, modern clubhouse, erected beside the Old England Hotel in 1964.

The advent of the steam engine and, later, the introduction of the internal combustion engine prompted the establishment, in 1925, of the Windermere Motor Boat Racing Club. 'Broadley's', the clubhouse, on the eastern side of the lake just north of Rawlinson Nab, is a masterpiece of Victorian architecture, designed in 1898 by C.F.A. Voysey in the style of the local vernacular revival. Throughout this early period, and well into the twentieth century, private boat ownership was beyond the means of all but the wealthiest of individuals, and the humbler classes who wished to enjoy a trip on the lake were confined to the steamers built by the Furness Railway Company, which today form the majestic 'Sealink' fleet. The oldest of the present boats is the *Tern*, built in 1891, whilst the *Swift* was launched in 1900, and the *Teal* and the *Swan* followed in 1936 and 1938 respectively. The smaller 'waterbuses', operated by the Bowness Bay Boating Company, are a more recent addition, the *Venture* being launched in 1966, and the first of the *Miss Cumbria* vessels being commissioned in 1974. The Esperance Pier, built originally for the private use of H.W. Schneider, now serves an ever-growing holiday traffic, and other piers have been erected nearby to cater for the expanding tourist trade.

For many years visitors have been able to hire rowing-boats from the more popular beaches along the shore, but the hire of cabin cruisers, and the development of holiday charter firms, is another more recent innovation based largely at Bowness. The 1960s and 70s have seen a proliferation in the number of moorings for private yachts and motor cruisers, including the building of the Windermere Marina to the south of Ferry Nab, together with the increasing number of chandlers and sailing-centres along the shores of Bowness Bay and at Waterhead.

Windermere has long been famous as a location where impressive records are set. The first person to swim the whole length of the lake was the Oldham swimming champion Joseph Foster, who completed his marathon swim on 2nd September 1911. Today the feat is regarded almost as commonplace, and an annual swimming race is held along the $10\frac{1}{2}$-mile course. In the early years of the century, Norman Buckley of Cragwood House held a number of world water-speed records on Windermere, while the summer of 1930 was marred by the tragic death of Sir Henry Seagrave and his engineer, who were killed whilst attempting to break the world water-speed record. In 1911 Captain E.W. Wakefield of Kendal became the first person to launch a seaplane into the air above Windermere, and by 1913 the Lakes Flying Company of Windermere were advertising flights in the *Water Hen*. During the Second World War Windermere became the home of the Sunderland Flying Boat Company, and the lake was regularly used to test the newly completed aircraft. The site of the factory, at White Cross Bay, is now occupied by a caravan site, and the temporary village erected at Low Wood to house the construction workers has subsequently been demolished.

Fame and recognition have also been brought upon Windermere and the surrounding countryside by the writings of several notable twentieth-century authors. Foremost among these literary celebrities is Beatrix Potter who in 1905 purchased Hill Top, a seventeenth-century farmhouse at Near Sawrey. Many of the adventures of Tom Kitten and his friends took place in and around Sawrey, and Beatrix Potter's *Journal*, written between 1881 and 1897, provides a refreshing picture of holidays spent in the Lake District before the noisy intrusion of the motor car. Arthur Ransome, who lived at Haverthwaite, managed to conjure up a marvellous picture of mysterious bays and lagoons in the adventures of the *Swallows and Amazons*, but, reading between the lines, a seasoned traveller can quickly recognize that 'Wild Cat Island' is firmly planted within the bounds of Windermere. The popularity of M.J.B. Baddeley's *Guide*, at the beginning of the century, was recorded by the erection of the Baddeley Memorial Clock, on the main road between Bowness and Windermere, in 1907, the year after the author died. Each of these writers has contributed greatly to the popularity of the Windermere landscape while, more recently, John Wyatt in *The Shining Levels* paints such a wistful picture of rural life in the woodlands surrounding the eastern shore that the reader yearns to climb amongst the crags and to witness with his own eyes the silvery sheen of the long, shining lake.

The popularity of the Windermere area developed during the early years of the century as the working classes of English society became more affluent and the working week became shorter. In the winter of 1895, and again in 1929, Windermere froze solid for several weeks, and the London and North Western Railway ran special weekend excursion trains from the bustling cities of Liverpool, Manchester and Lancaster. During the 1930s and 40s as many as seventeen excursion trains would discharge their passengers at Windermere Station on a typical Sunday at the height of the summer season, and both Bowness and Windermere expanded to cater for this growing influx. In 1892 a pavilion and a broad walk were constructed along the shore at Bowness Bay, while in 1912 these were replaced by the present gardens and Promenade. The digging of the foundations for the road alongside the Promenade revealed a mass grave to the south of St Martin's Churchyard, and ever since the road has been called 'Sepulchre Hill'.

By 1911 the resident population of Bowness and Windermere exceeded five thousand, and this figure was more than doubled in the summer by the hordes of day-trippers disgorged by the special excursion trains. After the end of the First World War, visitors arriving at Windermere Station could either walk the $1\frac{1}{2}$ miles along Lake Road to the shore at Bowness Bay or indulge in a ride on the new 'Magnet' motor omnibus. During the 1920s charabanc trips brought crowds of visitors to the lakeside, while touring the English Lakes by luxury coach gained in popularity after the Second World War. The most recent innovation in this field came with the setting-up of the Mountain Goat Minibus Company in 1972, based at Windermere and operating a number of summer services over narrow, steep routes such as the Kirkstone Pass and Little Langdale.

Throughout the earlier part of the twentieth century, large mansions such as Cragwood House and Brockhole continued to be constructed for businessmen and professional people who commuted daily by rail to Kendal, Lancaster, Liverpool or Manchester. By 1910 there were two early morning trains to Manchester or Liverpool. The Windermere Express departed first and was timetabled to complete the journey in just over two hours, while the later Club Train – the favourite with local businessmen – continued to make the daily journey until 1966. Saturday evening trips to Manchester or Liverpool catered for the regular theatre-goer, while the Lakes Express and three other daily trains to London ensured that the area was no longer an inaccessible rural backwater.

More recently the Windermere area has seen a great upsurge in the number of holiday and outdoor pursuits centres catering for the latest generation of active teenagers who come to develop skills in camping, canoeing, sailing, rock-climbing or orienteering. The setting-up of the Youth Hostels Association in the 1920s provided young people with an opportunity to explore the Lake District on a modest budget. Hostels at High Cross and Waterhead offer bed and breakfast at a very reasonable rate, while fell-walking and similar activities have been encouraged by the Ramblers' Association and by cheap accommodation provided by the YWCA, the Countrywide Holidays Association and the Holiday Fellowship. In 1936 an extensive area of woodland on the eastern shore of Windermere was presented to the Boy Scouts Association by Mr W.B. Wakeford, and Great Tower Plantation was opened as a national Scouts camping ground by Lord Baden-Powell. In 1953 the YMCA established their international camp on the western shore, near Lakeside, while more recently part of Storrs Hall has become the headquarters of the Central Council of Physical Recreation, and the Brathay estate has been converted into a residential outdoor pursuits centre by the Brathay Exploration Group. Several other large mansions, and other buildings, have been taken over by schools or local education authorities, and commercial ventures such as Fallbarrow Hall provide adventure holidays for a large number of young people.

With the development of all this bustling activity in the Windermere area, there has been a growing concern that the increasing popularity of the district might, at the least, detract from the peace and tranquillity which the majority seek here, or, at the worst, may cause irreversible damage to the very landscape that so many have come to admire. The growth of the local conservation movement can be traced back to early Victorian times, and Wordsworth's opposition to the Kendal and Windermere Railway in 1844 was only the first of many objections to major developments in the area. The Lake District Defence Association, founded to prevent the further expansion of the railway line beyond Windermere, became the forerunner of the National Trust, founded in 1895 by Canon Rawnsley, Vicar of Crosthwaite, together with several other local conservationists. The first major success of the Trust was its opposition to a proposal involving the construction of a 'light railway' or tramway along the shores of Windermere from Bowness to Ambleside. Since its inception, many benefactors have forwarded the aims of the conservation movement by donating buildings or estates to the National Trust, and today the Trust is one of the main landowners in the Lake District, owning over ninety thousand acres of fell and farmland. In the Bowness area, Queen Adelaide's Hill was acquired in 1913 and

Post Knott in 1929, while Cockshott Point was purchased by public subscription in 1937 and handed over to the Trust for safe-keeping. Beatrix Potter was a great supporter of the Trust and not only purchased many farms on the surrounding fells but also bequeathed her home at Hill Top, Near Sawrey, on her death. Other National Trust properties include Borran's Field, Hawkshead Courthouse, Storrs Temple and Wray Castle, while Fell Foot – formerly the home of the Ridehalghs of Staveley – was opened as a lakeside leisure centre in 1973. The National Trust operates a policy of open access to the public wherever possible, and nature trails have been laid out through Skelghyll Woods, along the shore below Claife Heights and at White Moss Common.

The idea of a national park in the Windermere area can again be traced back over a hundred years. Wordsworth, writing in the middle of the nineteenth century, favoured the creation of 'a sort of national property in which every man has a right and interest', while W.G. Collingwood, pondering the idea in 1925, suggested, 'Whether a people's park is really wanted, the people must decide. A modest something of the sort is still possible in the Western half of the Lake District.'

Wordsworth's dream became a reality in 1951 when the National Parks Commission, set up in 1949, designated the Lake District as the largest of ten national parks to be established in England and Wales. These ten parks were created 'for the purpose of preserving and enhancing the natural beauty of the areas', and although the Lake District National Park Authority owns very little land in the Windermere area, it has probably had more direct effect upon the recent development of the landscape than has any other single body. The Lake District National Park, covering some 866 square miles of the Cumbrian Mountains, is administered by the Lake District Special Planning Board, who also act as the planning authority for the whole of the national park – a function usually shared by the county council and the local district councils. The Board fulfils its commission by pursuing three main aims: the preservation of the beauty of the landscape, the provision of facilities for its enjoyment, and the welfare of the local economy and the local population.

The most obvious manifestation of these policies is the provision of a wide range of facilities designed to help visitors in the understanding and appreciation of the landscape. The measures adopted include the building of car-parks and picnic areas, such as those at Beech Hill and Rayrigg Meadow, and the opening of the country's first National Park Centre at Brockhole in 1969. Brockhole was originally built as a fine lakeside mansion by William Henry Gaddum, a Manchester businessman, in 1899, and the gardens were laid out by Thomas Mawson, a landscape gardener from Windermere. The formal lawns and terraced gardens near the house give way to open parkland, before reaching out to the cultivated wilderness of Birkett Wood, by the lake shore. The property became a convalescent home after Gaddum's death in 1945 and was purchased by the national park authority in 1966. Today it contains a comprehensive display, providing the visitor with a fascinating introduction to the Lakeland landscape, as well as housing a small lecture theatre, a reference library, a café and picnic areas.

The National Park Information Service also provides a number of smaller information centres in the Windermere area, including the information bureau at Waterhead and the countryside theatre at Bowness Bay. The information centre at Ambleside Court House occupies part of the old 1882 police station, vacated by the local constabulary on the opening of the modern police station at Rydal Road. The national park authority also encourages free public access to the countryside by the waymarking of public footpaths and the maintenance of stiles and gateways. Occasionally, to preserve, or to create, free access to an area, the authority has purchased small patches of public access land, including nine of the islands of Windermere and seventy acres of land at High Dam, on Finsthwaite Heights.

In pursuing a policy of support for the local agricultural economy, the national park authority has set up an Upland Management Service, to minimize the inconvenience and loss caused to local farmers as a result of the promotion of tourist activities. The Upland Management Service is co-ordinated by a team of full-time rangers and voluntary wardens who organize parties to carry out litter sweeps, to repair damage to stone walls and to discourage dogs from roaming the fells freely during lambing times.

The third responsibility of the Lake District Special Planning Board is to preserve the beauty and the special character of the area, whilst at the same time encouraging its enjoyment by the public at large. These two aims are often in direct conflict with each other, and the national park authority – in its role as the local planning authority – is required to be particularly sympathetic and sensitive to the needs of the district. In its *Policy for Tourism*, published in 1966, the authority recognized that 'the tourist industry must be promoted and conducted so as not to impair ... the special character and quality of the district', and 'it would therefore be a mistaken policy to attract into the National Park those whose tastes are for gregarious holiday making and urban gaiety by providing the more organized amusement appropriate to the larger holiday resorts'. These warnings, reminiscent of Wordsworth's foreboding over a century ago, have led to the development of policies which seek to preserve the Lakeland landscape as an area for quiet recreation and peaceful rehabilitation.

During the 1970s the Special Planning Board was a party to the preparation of the 'Cumbria County Structure Plan' and the 'Lake District National Park Plan', both of which entailed detailed public consultation before the final versions were authorized for publication. One of the chief problems faced by the planners in the preparation of these documents has been the excessive demands made by tourism – especially at peak holiday periods – on the roads, on the residential facilities and on the lake itself.

Congestion on the narrow roads of the Lake District, especially at Bank Holiday weekends, first became an acutely serious problem as the trend towards universal car-ownership steadily accelerated during the 1950s. With the opening of the M6 motorway and the Kendal Bypass, during the 1960s, over twenty million people have been brought within a three-hour drive of the shores of Windermere, and the decline of the railways has done little to alleviate the mounting pressure on the roads. The Lakeside branch of the railway was closed in 1965 as part of the Beeching rationalization plan, though the $3\frac{1}{2}$-mile section between Haverthwaite and Lakeside was subsequently reopened as a tourist attraction by a group of steam enthusiasts in 1970. On the Windermere line, services were progressively reduced throughout the 1960s, and in 1972 only fourteen excursion trains arrived at Windermere Station during the whole of the summer season. In 1973 the line was reduced to a single track, and the failure to electrify the route at the same time as the main line has meant that it is now impossible to operate locomotive-hauled excursions directly to Windermere.

Ironically, the fuel crisis of 1974 led to the overcrowding of the remaining rail services, and increasing concern was voiced by the 'Friends of the Lake District' over the additional pressure being borne by the roads. The policy adopted by the Lake District Special Planning Board has been one of compromise: widening the main through routes such as the A591 between Kendal and Windermere but preserving the character of the winding side roads and preventing their misuse by heavy vehicles with the imposition of width restrictions on the narrowest routes. Heavy traffic has also been discouraged from using the main A591 as a through route between Kendal and Keswick, by the introduction of a ban on heavy goods vehicles across Dunmail Raise, to the north of Ambleside.

A further conflict involved in preserving the beauty of the countryside has been the increasing demand for residential facilities, especially the provision of camping and caravan sites, and the influx of city-dwellers desiring a second home. The national park authority has tried hard to restrict the development of camping and caravan sites to locations that are well shielded by trees, and the construction of a large and exposed camp-site on the floor of the Troutbeck valley was the subject of much local opposition. Of equal concern to local residents is the inflationary effect on local house prices resulting from the purchase of second homes and holiday cottages by wealthy individuals residing in other parts of the country. Although this phenomenon is nothing new to the area, the increasing affluence of the nation during the 1950s and 60s exacerbated the problem to the extent that many young people who have grown up in the Windermere area are now forced to move away as they cannot afford to live there. The problem is being met by the building of local authority housing and the encouragement of housing society projects, while restrictive-purchasing clauses are increasingly being forced upon speculative property developers. Rigorous planning restrictions are imposed upon *any* new development, including stipulations on the use of local building materials, controls on the height of multi-storey buildings, and regulations concerning the colour of paintwork and the external appearance of the property. Despite the concern of the local population, some of the smaller villages in the Windermere area are rapidly becoming dying communities, as an increasing proportion of the village residences are occupied only at holiday times. This in turn has an unfavourable effect on the provision of local services, and many smaller settlements are facing, or have already suffered, the closure of their village shop, the decline of the village school or the withdrawal of their local bus service.

Perhaps the most pressing problem facing the planning authority is the over-use of the lake itself. The Windermere Recreation Survey, carried out in 1977, recorded as many as 750 boats active on the lake at the same time on a fine Sunday in August. Over seventy of these craft were fast sports boats engaged in the activity of water-skiing – a sport which can be very hazardous to other lake-users. The report recommended the zoning of recreational activities, and since that date water-skiing, for example, has become restricted to certain parts of the lake. The dangers of speedboats navigating the same waters as rowing-boats has led to the imposition of speed limits on the northern and southern reaches of the lake and in the congested area around Bowness Bay, while registration of all boats using the lake and an increasing vigilance by the lake wardens have assisted in the enforcement of these safety regulations. Although the lake bed is owned by the local authority – having been presented to Windermere UDC in 1939 by Alderman H.L. Groves, the High Sheriff of Westmorland – the general public are free to use the lake at any time, provided that all boats are launched at a recognized public or privately owned landing site. The over-use of Windermere, especially by motor cruisers and fast sports boats, prompted the national park authority to introduce bye-laws in 1974 prohibiting the use of any motor-powered vessel on twenty of the smaller tarns and lakes in the area, including Esthwaite Water, Blelham Tarn, High Dam and Loughrigg Tarn. A constant watch is being kept on the use of Windermere itself, and only time will tell whether further restrictions may become necessary.

While the trappings of twentieth-century commercial tourism threaten to engulf the very peace and calm which most visitors come to find, a healthy economy in the Windermere area relies not only upon tourism but also upon the maintenance of a viable agriculture and on job opportunities provided for the local population by forestry, industry and tertiary activities.

During the twentieth century local agriculture has seen an increase in the tendency towards larger and more efficient farm units. On the fellsides and in the valley floors, smallholdings have been consolidated into larger units, and redundant farmhouses and barns have been purchased by townsfolk and converted into luxury villas or *bijou* residences. The fells have been converted into large sheep-ranches and stocked with herds of Swaledale or Rough Fell sheep, though on the farms owned by the National Trust it is still customary to 'let' flocks of heave-going sheep together with the hill farms, as the flocks become acclimatized to the area and have a strong homing instinct. Most of the stock is grazed on the open fell throughout the year, though pregnant ewes may be wintered on the inby land near the farmstead and then transferred to intake land during the summer. Conditions are often bleak, and a particularly bad winter – such as that of 1947 – can result in the death of thousands of sheep. The rough grassland is not ideal for fattening the lambs, and most of the stock is sold to lowland farmers on reaching the local livestock markets.

On the valley floors, and beside the lake, rural electrification schemes have enabled farmers to install automatic milking parlours, and the setting-up of the Milk Marketing Board in 1933 provided a ready market for supplies of liquid milk. Herds of Friesian cattle provide the most economic return for lake-side farmsteads, and grazing on fertile inby land is supplemented in the winter by stall-feeding on silage or artificial concentrates.

Agriculture remains viable in this rather marginal area by the valuable provision of government subsidies for hill-farmers. These payments, however, do not benefit only the farmers themselves, for agriculture directly assists the tourist industry by keeping the countryside attractive and by preventing the spread of collapsing walls and derelict farm buildings. In its turn, tourism helps the farmers by providing additional income from bed and breakfast or by enabling a farmer to use a field or two as a temporary camping site.

A further boost to tourism came with the realization, during the 1960s and 70s, that the nation's forests could also be used as a great recreational resource. The Forestry Commission was originally established, in 1919, with the intention of building up a strategic reserve of timber, following the large-scale fellings during the First World War. The most extensive Forestry Commission plantations in the Windermere area are found on the western shore at Grizedale Forest. Grizedale Hall was built in 1903 for the millionaire Harold Brocklebank but was demolished after the Grizedale Hall Estate was purchased by the Forestry Commission in 1937. At that time the estate consisted of seven farms, with much rough open fell country and a small area of sessile oak woodland. The Commission sold one of the existing farms and amalgamated the remaining holdings into two larger and two smaller farms, occupying most of the more fertile land on the valley floor. The remaining fell country was planted with 6,616 acres of coniferous trees, mostly Sitka spruce and Japanese larch, though the actual species planted depended on the local conditions. Sitka spruce and Scots pine were planted on the degraded sheep-walks and on the more rocky areas, while Japanese larch was preferred on the bracken-covered slopes, and Norway spruce or Douglas fir were planted on the better soils. Today the forest yields over seven thousand tons of timber per annum, and the eventual yield, as the forest matures, should reach over three times this amount. Most of the wood is used for pulp and paper, though thinnings are used for posts and stakes, and a smaller proportion of the crop is used for constructional timber.

As the Forestry Commission expanded its operations in this area, and many acres of former open fell country were fenced off to protect the seedlings from the attention of browsing animals, there was a growing concern that the landscape of the Lake District was being irreversibly ruined by the unsympathetic planting of vast areas of conifers. In order to counter the growing fears of the public, the Forestry Commission entered into an informal agreement with the Council for the Preservation of Rural England, in 1936, whereby it agreed not to purchase any land for afforestation in the central three hundred square miles of the Lake District. This area includes land bordering the Windermere valley, and it is unlikely that any further large-scale plantings will take place here.

Even more significant for the country-going public has been a marked change in the official policy of the Forestry Commission, which has led to the opening-up of the forests to the public and has encouraged their use for recreational purposes. Far from discouraging visitors, the Forestry Commission now actively promotes the enjoyment of Grizedale Forest by laying out walks and nature trails, by an interpretative display and by the provision of a restaurant and Theatre-in-the-Forest. The Millwood Forest Trail winds through the older woodlands in the vicinity of the Grizedale forestry centre, while the Silurian Way is a long-distance way-marked route which explores the remoter parts of the more recent plantations. During the winter the forest access roads are sometimes used by car-rally enthusiasts, and for several years crowds have been attracted to the forest as the RAC Rally has passed this way. The Commission also encourages the maintenance of wildlife areas, with nesting boxes for birds and observation hides to enable visitors to catch a glimpse of the herd of native red deer. The greylag goose has been re-introduced on some of the existing tarns, and provision has been made for angling on Grizedale Beck. The emphasis has switched from the exclusive production of timber to a concept of multiple land-use, and the area has been enriched as a result of the wealth of recreational pursuits which have been encouraged.

Another recent development which at first attracted great opposition – but which has since become an accepted feature of the district – is the use of Windermere for water storage by the North West Water Authority. Schemes for the abstraction of water from the lakes of Cumbria are nothing new, the first of these schemes dating back to 1876 when the Manchester Corporation Water Works converted Thirlmere into a reservoir. Early projects such as those at Thirlmere and Haweswater have been criticized for their artificial, fluctuating shorelines and their unsightly dams, and it was with some relief that the proposal to create an artificial reservoir by drowning the Winster valley was defeated during the 1960s. The Windermere project, however, is quite different in conception and has made very little visible difference to the landscape. Water is pumped out of the lake from a depth of sixty feet below the surface via an underground pumping station, carefully concealed beneath a grassy mound near Troutbeck Bridge. From here, an aqueduct carries the water to the Watchgate treatment works, near Kendal, where it is chlorinated, together with supplies from Haweswater. Work on the project began in 1971, and the water authority is now able to extract 45 million gallons of water per day, while promising not to allow the water level to drop below 128 feet above sea level.

The Windermere area has few extractive or manufacturing industries. Quarrying has all but ceased in the vicinity, and the old quay which handled sand and gravel dredged from the bed of Windermere was closed in 1975 to make way for the Steamboat Museum. An older sand wharf on the south side of Bowness Bay is now occupied by moorings for motor cruisers, whilst the adjoining site, formerly occupied by a series of Victorian boat houses, is now dominated by Shepherd's 'Aquarius' Restaurant and the adjacent boatbuilding workshops, erected in 1974. The former railway sidings at Windermere Station are now occupied by the premises of a firm manufacturing plastic containers, while local craftsmen produce pottery, jewellery, leatherwork and wood-carvings for the seasonal tourist trade.

The majority of the local population, however, are employed in tertiary occupations, such as postmen, firemen, doctors or teachers. Windermere became an important research centre with the establishment of the Freshwater Biological Association at Ferry House in 1948, while it also serves an important educational role with the Lakes School, the Charlotte Mason College of Education and the Merchant Navy training college at Wray Castle – all within a short walk of its shores.

If we look forward to the twenty-first century, it is becoming increasingly evident that the preservation of the Windermere landscape can take place only within the context of a viable local economy. Although the region has a beauty and a unique character which should be maintained at all costs, it is clear that the variety in the landscape is largely the result of man's handiwork, brought about over numerous centuries by the practical needs of a changing local economy. In the remaining years of the twentieth century, the local economy will undoubtedly continue to change as the nation moves hesitatingly towards the unknown horizons of a post-industrial society. As the economy changes, so too will the demands made on the Lakeland landscape. In this situation, it would be foolish to imagine that the landscape as we see it today will never alter; all we can hope for is that the changes which will inevitably occur may be sympathetic to the existing character of the area and that inappropriate developments may never be allowed to spoil the beauty of the Windermere landscape.

Bibliography

Abbreviations

CW2 Transactions of the Cumberland and Westmorland
      Antiquarian and Archaeological Society
(OS) Old Series, Vols I – XVI (1866-1900)
(NS) New Series, Vol. I (1901) and subsequent annual volumes

General

Bouch, C.M.L. and Jones, G.P. *A short Economic and Social
    History of the Lake Counties, 1500-1830* (Manchester, 1961)
Millward, R. and Robinson, A. *The Lake District,* The Regions
    of Britain (London, 1970)
Millward, R. and Robinson, A. *Cumbria*, Landscapes of Britain
    (London, 1972)

Chapter 1: 'The Windermere Landscape'

Davies-Shiel, M. 'The Making of Potash for Soap in Lakeland',
    CW2 (NS), LXXII (1972), 85-111
Kipling, C. 'The Commercial Fisheries of Windermere', *CW2*
    (NS), LXXII (1972), 156-204
Pearsall, W.H. and Pennington, W. *The Lake District*, New
    Naturalist Series (London, 1973)
West, T. *A Guide to the Lakes in Cumberland, Westmorland
    and Lancashire* (London, 1778)

Wordsworth, W. *A Complete Guide to the Lakes* (London, 1835, reprinted 1970)
Wordsworth, W. *The Poetical Works of William Wordsworth* (London, 1850)

Chapter 2: 'Exploring the Windermere Landscape'

Lake District National Park Information Service. *A Walking Route between Bowness and Hawkshead*.
National Trust. *A Lake-Shore Walk: the Claife Shore of Windermere*
National Trust. *A Nature Walk at White Moss Common, Rydal*
Wainwright, A. *The Outlying Fells of Lakeland* (Kendal, 1974)
Wilson, J. *Recreations of Christopher North*, Vol. I (London, 1887)

Chapter 3: 'Rocks, Rivers and Ice'

Gresswell, R.K. 'The glacial geomorphology of the south-eastern part of the Lake District', *Liverpool and Manchester Geological Journal*, 1 (1951), 57-70
Macan, T.T. *Biological Studies of the English Lakes* (London, 1970)
Marr, J.E. *The Geology of the Lake District* (Cambridge, 1916, reprinted Bath, 1968)
Moseley, F. (ed.) *The Geology of the Lake District*, Yorkshire Geological Society Occasional Publication No. 3 (Leeds, 1978)
Otley, J. 'Remarks on the Succession of Rocks, in the District of the Lakes', *Lonsdale Magazine*, 1 (1820), 433-5
Otley, J. *A Descriptive Guide to The English Lakes, and Adjacent Mountains* (Keswick, 1823)
Pennington, W. 'Studies of the post-glacial history of British vegetation. VII. Lake Sediments: pollen diagrams from the bottom deposits of the North basin of Windermere', *Philosophical Transactions of the Royal Society*, B, 233 (1947), 137-75
Pennington, W. 'The recent sediments of Windermere',

Freshwater Biology, 3 (1973), 363-82

Shackleton, E.H. *Lakeland Geology* (Clapham, 1966)

Chapter 4: 'Early Settlers'

Burkett, M.E. 'Recent Discoveries at Ambleside', *CW2* (NS), LXV (1965), 86-101

Collingwood, R.G. *Ambleside Roman Fort* (Ambleside, 1965) (4th Ed.)

Cowper, H.S. 'Some prehistoric remains in North Lonsdale', *CW2* (OS), IX (1885-7), 200-205

Eckwall, E. *The Concise Oxford Dictionary of English Place Names* (Oxford, 1960) (4th Ed.)

Lowndes, R.A.C. 'Allen Knott earthwork', *CW2* (NS), LXIV (1964), 94-7

Plint, R.G. 'Stone Axe factory sites in the Cumbrian fells', *CW2* (NS), LXII (1962), 1-26

Royal Commission on Historical Monuments – England. *An Inventory of the Historical Monuments in Westmorland* (London, 1936)

Williams, I. *The Poems of Taliesin,* translated by J.E.C. Williams (Dublin, 1968)

Chapter 5: 'Norse and Normans'

Kirby, D.P. 'Strathclyde and Cumbria: a survey of historical development to 1092', *CW2* (NS), LXII (1962), 77-94

Oldfield, F. 'Pollen Analysis and man's role in the ecological history of the South-East Lake District', *Geografiska Annaler*, 45 (1963), 23-40

Smith, A.H. *The Place-Names of Westmorland*, Vol. XLII of the English Place-Name Society (Cambridge, 1967)

Wilson, P.A. 'On the use of the terms "Strathclyde" and "Cumbria" ', *CW2* (NS), LXVI (1966), 57-92

Chapter 6: 'Furness Abbey and Medieval Industries'

Armitt, M.L. 'Fullers and Freeholders of the Parish of
    Grasmere', *CW2* (NS), VIII (1908), 136-205
Brownbill, J. (Ed.) *The Coucher Book of Furness Abbey*, 3 vols,
    Chetham Society (Manchester, 1915-19)
Collingwood, W.G. *Lake District History* (Kendal, 1925)
Collingwood, W.G. 'The medieval fence of Rydal and other
    linear earthworks', *CW2* (NS), XXX (1930), 1-11
Davies-Shiel, M. 'The Ash Burners', *CW2* (NS), LXXIV (1974),
    33-64
Davies-Shiel, M. *Wool is my Bread* (Kendal, 1975)
Nicholson, J. and Burn, R. *The History and Antiquities of the
    Counties of Westmorland and Cumberland* (London, 1777,
    reprinted East Ardsley, 1976)
Pennington, W. 'Pollen Analysis from six upland tarns in the
    Lake District', *Philosophical Transactions of the Royal
    Society*, B, 248 (1968), 204-44

Chapter 7: 'Yeoman Farmers and Market Towns'

Armitt, M.L. 'Ambleside Town and Chapel', *CW2* (NS), VI
    (1906), 1-96
Beck, T.A. *Annales Furnesienses: History and Antiquities of the
    Abbey of Furness* (London, 1844)
Brunskill, R.W. *Vernacular Architecture of the Lake Counties*
    (London, 1974)
Davies-Shiel, M. and Marshall, J.D. *The Industrial Archaeology
    of the Lake Counties* (Newton Abbot, 1969, reprinted
    Beckermet, 1977)
Griffiths, E.W. (Ed.) *Through England on a side saddle in the
    time of William and Mary, being the diary of Celia Fiennes*
    (London, 1888)
Kipling, C. 'The netting sites of Windermere', *CW2* (NS),
    LXXIII (1973), 111-19
Kipling, C. 'Some documentary evidence on woodlands in
    the vicinity of Windermere', *CW2*, (NS), LXXIV (1974), 65-88
Marshall, J.D. 'The domestic economy of the Lakeland

yeoman, 1660-1749', *CW2* (NS), LXXIII (1973), 190-219

Somervell, J. *Some Westmorland Wills 1686-1738* (Kendal, 1928)

Chapter 8: 'The Romantic Age'

Baddeley, M.J.B. *The English Lake District*, Thorough Guide Series (London, 1886)

Garnett, F.W. *Westmorland Agriculture 1800-1900* (Kendal, 1912)

Gilpin, W. *Observations on the Mountains, and Lakes of Cumberland, and Westmorland* (London, 1772)

Gray, T. 'Journal of a Tour in the Lakes', in Toynbee, P. and Whibley, L. (Eds) *Correspondence of Thomas Gray*, 3 vols (Oxford, 1935)

Jones, G.P. 'The decline of the yeomanry in the Lake District', *CW2* (NS), LXII (1962), 198-223

Murray, J. *Handbook of the English Lakes* (London, 1867)

Pringle, A. *General view of the Agriculture of the county of Westmorland* (Edinburgh, 1794)

Stockdale, J. *Annals of Cartmel* (Ulverston, 1872)

Wainwright, A. *A Pictorial Guide to the Lakeland Fells*, 7 vols (Kendal, 1955-66)

Wilkinson, J. *Select Views in Cumberland, Westmorland and Lancashire* (London, 1810)

Young, A. *A Six Months' Tour through the North of England* (London, 1770)

Chapter 9: 'The Coming of the Railways'

Cowper, H.S. *Hawkshead: Its History, Archaeology, Industries, Folklore and Dialect* (London, 1899)

Hunt, I. *The Lakeland Pedlar* (Ulverston, 1977)

Marshall, J.D. and Davies-Shiel, M. *Victorian and Edwardian Lake District from old photographs* (London, 1976)

Martineau, H. *Complete Guide to the English Lakes* (Windermere, 1855)

Mellentin, J. *Kendal and Windermere Railway* (Clapham, 1980)

Parson, W. and White, W. *A History, Directory and Gazeteer of Cumberland and Westmorland with Furness and Cartmel* (Leeds, 1829, reprinted Beckermet, 1976)

Quayle, H.I. and Jenkins, S.C. *Lakeside and Haverthwaite Railway* (Clapham, 1977)

Thompson, B.L. *The Parish Church of St Martin, Windermere: A History and Guide* (Windermere, 1966)

Chapter 10: 'The Twentieth Century'

Cumbria County Council and Lake District Special Planning Board. *Cumbria and Lake District Joint Structure Plan: Written Statement* (Carlisle, 1980)

Lake District Special Planning Board. *Lake District National Park Plan* (Kendal, 1978)

Lake Windermere Steering Committee. *Windermere Recreation Survey, 1977* (Kendal, 1978)

Lake Windermere Steering Committee. *Windermere: A Management Plan for the Lake* (Kendal, 1980)

Potter, B. *The Journal of Beatrix Potter, 1881-97* (London, 1966)

Ransome, A. *Swallows and Amazons* (London, 1930)

Wyatt, J. *The Shining Levels* (London, 1973)

Index